D0485436

# ENGLISH LANGUAGE
## SUPER REVIEW®

By the Staff of
Research & Education Association

**Research & Education Association**
Visit our website at: www.rea.com

***Research & Education Association***
61 Ethel Road West
Piscataway, New Jersey 08854
E-mail: info@rea.com

# ENGLISH LANGUAGE
# SUPER REVIEW®

**Published 2017**
Copyright © 2000 by Research & Education Association, Inc.

Printed in the United States of America

Library of Congress Control Number 00-130281

ISBN-13: 978-0-87891-186-8
ISBN-10: 0-87891-186-3

SUPER REVIEW® and REA® are registered trademarks
of Research & Education Association, Inc.

**If you're looking for a handy guide to help you master the basics of English grammar and usage, this is the book for you!**

Whether you need a study companion for a grammar class or a reference at work, REA's *English Language Super Review®* gives you everything you need to know.

This *Super Review®* can be used as a supplement to your high school or college textbook, or as a handy guide any time you need a fast review of the subject.

Here you'll find:

- **Comprehensive yet concise coverage** with simple guidelines for improving your spelling, understanding the parts of speech, avoiding common grammar and punctuation errors, and dealing with frequently confused and misused words.

- **Questions and answers for each topic** designed to reinforce what you've learned.

- **End-of-chapter quizzes** let you check your progress every step of the way. You'll be speaking and writing better before you know it.

When you need to brush up your grammar and usage with confidence, we think you'll agree that REA's *Super Review®* provides everything you need!

# Available Super Review® Titles

## ARTS/HUMANITIES
Basic Music
Classical Mythology
History of Architecture
History of Greek Art

## BUSINESS
Accounting
Macroeconomics
Microeconomics

## COMPUTER SCIENCE
C++
Java

## HISTORY
Canadian History
European History
United States History

## LANGUAGES
English
French
French Verbs
Italian
Japanese for Beginners
Japanese Verbs
Latin
Spanish

## MATHEMATICS
Algebra & Trigonometry
Basic Math & Pre-Algebra
Calculus
Geometry
Linear Algebra
Pre-Calculus
Statistics

## SCIENCES
Anatomy & Physiology
Biology
Chemistry
Entomology
Geology
Microbiology
Organic Chemistry I & II
Physics

## SOCIAL SCIENCES
Psychology I & II
Sociology

## WRITING
College & University Writing

# About REA

Founded in 1959, Research & Education Association is dedicated to publishing the finest and most effective educational materials—including study guides and test preps—for students of all ages.

Today, REA's wide-ranging catalog is a leading resource for students, teachers, and other professionals. Visit *www.rea.com* to see a complete listing of all our titles.

# Acknowledgments

We would like to thank Pam Weston, Publisher, for setting the quality standards for production integrity and managing the publication to completion; Larry B. Kling, Vice President, Editorial, for his supervision of revisions and overall direction; and Jennifer Calhoun, Graphic Designer, for designing our cover.

# Contents

**Chapter 1  The Noun**.................................................. 1
    1.1    Nouns ...........................................................1
    1.2    Concrete and Abstract Nouns...........................4
    1.3    Collective Nouns............................................4
    1.4    Countable and Noncountable Nouns .....................4
    1.5    Noun Compounds .........................................6
    1.6    Gender.......................................................7
    1.7    Number–Plural Nouns ...................................8
    1.8    The Possessive Case......................................10

**Chapter 2  Pronouns** ...............................................22
    2.1    Types of Pronouns ......................................22
    2.2    Case–The Function of the
           Pronoun in a Sentence ................................33
    2.3    *Who* and *Whom* ..........................................40
    2.4    *Whoever* and *Whomever* ...............................42
    2.5    Agreement.................................................43
    2.6    Reference Pronouns .....................................45

**Chapter 3  Expletives** ..............................................49
    3.1    It ............................................................49
    3.2    There .......................................................50

**Chapter 4  Verbs** ....................................................52
    4.1    Kinds of Verbs ...........................................52
    4.2    Forms of English Verbs.................................59
    4.3    Tense.......................................................60
    4.4    Regular and Irregular Verbs...........................64

4.5 Agreement Between Subjects and Verbs ................73
4.6 Verbals ........................................................78
4.7 Voice ...........................................................81
4.8 Mood............................................................83
Quiz: **The Noun, Pronouns, Expletives and Verbs** .......84

**Chapter 5 Adjectives and Adverbs** ...............................87
5.1 Recognizing Adjectives and Adverbs .....................87
5.2 Degrees of Adjectives and Adverbs .......................90
5.3 Comparison with "Other" or "Else" or "Of All" .......95
5.4 Confusion with Adverbs and Adjectives .................95
5.5 Faulty Comparisons ........................................97

**Chapter 6 Prepositions**.............................................99
6.1 Simple Prepositions.........................................99
6.2 Group Prepositions..........................................100
6.3 Idiomatic Use of Prepositions.............................102
6.4 List of Common Prepositions ..............................103

**Chapter 7 Conjunctions** ...........................................105
7.1 Coordinating Conjunctions .................................105
7.2 Conjunctive Adverbs ........................................107
7.3 Correlative Conjunctions (used in pairs) .............109
7.4 Subordinating Conjunctions ...............................110
Quiz: **Adjectives & Adverbs, Prepositions,**
      **and Conjunctions** ...................................112

**Chapter 8 Parts of the Sentence** .................................116
8.1 Subject and Predicate.......................................116
8.2 Sentence Order ..............................................118

**Chapter 9  Phrases** ...................................................121
   9.1    Prepositional Phrases......................................121
   9.2    Gerund Phrases ..............................................123
   9.3    Infinitive Phrases ...........................................124
   9.4    Participal Phrases ..........................................125
   9.5    Absolute Phrases ...........................................126

**Chapter 10  Clauses**.................................................128
   10.1   Independent and Subordinate Clauses .................128
   10.2   Elliptical Clauses...........................................130
   **Quiz: Parts of the Sentence, Phrases,
        and Clauses**........................................... 131

**Chapter 11  Sentence Errors–Structural Problems** ........134
   11.1   Dangling Modifiers.........................................134
   11.2   Misplaced Modifiers.......................................135
   11.3   Lack of Parallel Structure ...............................137
   11.4   Sentence Fragments .......................................140
   11.5   Run-On Sentences..........................................142
   11.6   Comma Splices ..............................................142
   11.7   Short, Choppy Sentences–Sentence Variation ......144
   11.8   Wordiness.....................................................145
   11.9   Rambling Sentences .......................................146

**Chapter 12  Glossary of Usage**..................................147
   12.1   Words Commonly Confused and Misused...........147
   **Quiz: Sentence Errors–Structural Problems
        and Glossary of Usage**..................................154

**Chapter 13 End Punctuation Marks**......................................158

   13.1   The Period ...............................................158

   13.2   The Question Mark ..................................160

   13.3   The Exclamation Point ...........................161

**Chapter 14 Internal Punctuation Marks**............................164

   14.1   The Comma..............................................164

   14.2   The Semicolon .......................................171

   14.3   The Colon ...............................................174

   14.4   The Dash..................................................177

   14.5   Parentheses ............................................178

   14.6   Quotation Marks.....................................179

   14.7   The Apostrophe.......................................185

   14.8   Italics.......................................................187

   14.9   Hyphens ..................................................189

   14.10 Brackets ..................................................191

   14.11 Ellipsis ....................................................192

   Quiz: End Punctuation Marks and
          Internal Punctuation Marks ...............................193

**Chapter 15 Numbers**.............................................................196

   15.1   Over 100 and Under 100..........................196

   15.2   Ordinal Numbers and Fractions.............197

   15.3   Addresses ...............................................197

   15.4   Dates.......................................................198

   15.5   Parts of a Book........................................198

   15.6   Plural Forms............................................198

**Chapter 16  Capitalization**....................................................200

  16.1    Proper Nouns.............................................200

  16.2    Sentences and Sentence Fragments .....................203

  16.3    Sentences Within Sentences.................................203

  16.4    Lines of Poetry .......................................................203

  16.5    Titles of Works.......................................................203

  **Quiz: Numbers and Capitalization** .............................205


**Chapter 17  Spelling** ...............................................................208

  17.1    Word Analysis .........................................................208

  17.2    Spelling List.............................................................210

  17.3    Spelling Rules..........................................................211

  17.4    Proofreading ...........................................................216

  **Quiz: Spelling** .................................................................217

# CHAPTER 1

# The Noun

## 1.1 Nouns

A **noun** is a part of speech that names a person, place, thing, idea, animal, quality, or action. Along with verbs, nouns are the principal elements of any sentence.

Into each *life* some *rain* must fall.

On his *vacation* in *California*, *Jason* called his *sister*.

*John* gave the *men* their *money* for the *work*.

All the italicized words in the above sentences are examples of nouns. Just as people can be classified according to a number of characteristics, such as hair color, height, weight, occupation, income, or nationality, so can nouns be classified according to specific characteristics.

## Problem Solving Example:

Identify which of the following words are nouns by writing Yes or No in the blank provided.

a. _____ clock

b. _____ begin

c. _____ fish

d. _____ Poland

e. _____ large

f. _____ ice

a. *Clock* is a noun.

b. *Begin* is not a noun. *Begin* is a verb.

c. *Fish* is a noun.

d. *Poland* is a noun.

e. *Large* is not a noun. *Large* is an adjective.

f. *Ice* is a noun.

Most nouns are **common nouns**. They name any one of a class or kind of people, places, or things. A **proper noun** is the official name of a particular person, place, or thing. The writer's main problem with proper nouns is recognizing them so they can be capitalized (see *Capitalization*).

Proper nouns include the following:

### Personal names

| | |
|---|---|
| Mr. William Jones | Susan Lee Gray |
| Dr. Harrison | Captain Smith |
| John Mills, Jr. | Mrs. Laurence |
| Zeus | St. Francis |
| Pope Paul | President Roosevelt |

### Names of Nationalities and Religions

| | |
|---|---|
| Frenchman | Judaism |
| Englishman | Catholicism |

### Geographic Names

| | |
|---|---|
| Paris | Seine River |
| New York City | England |

|  |  |
|---|---|
| Beijing | Mount Wilson |

### Names of Holidays

|  |  |
|---|---|
| Christmas | Rosh Hashanah |
| Columbus Day | Thanksgiving Day |

### Names of Time Units

|  |  |
|---|---|
| Monday | February |

## Problem Solving Example:

 Identify whether the underlined words are common or proper nouns.

a. Linda celebrated <u>Memorial Day</u> at <u>Myrtle Beach</u> this <u>year</u>.

b. <u>John Keats</u>, an English <u>poet</u>, wrote "Ode on a Grecian Urn."

c. In my comparative <u>religion</u> class, I studied <u>Buddhism</u>, Hinduism, Judaism, Catholicism, and Christianity.

d. The Dutch student visited an <u>art gallery</u> near <u>Lake Michigan</u>.

e. Professor Haven has office hours on <u>Tuesday</u> and Thursday <u>mornings</u>.

 a. *Memorial Day* is a proper noun. *Memorial Day* is a holiday. *Myrtle Beach* is a proper noun. It is a geographic place. *Year* is a common noun.

b. *John Keats* is a proper noun. *John Keats* is a personal name. *Poet* is a common noun.

c. *Buddhism* is a proper noun. It is the name of a religion. *Religion* is a common noun.

d. *Lake Michigan* is a proper noun. It is a geographic place. *Art gallery* is a common noun.

e. *Tuesday* is a proper noun. It is a unit of time. *Mornings* is a common noun.

## 1.2 Concrete and Abstract Nouns

A noun that names a member of a class, a group of people, places, or things is a **concrete noun,** because what it names is physical, visible, and tangible. Examples of concrete nouns are book and rose. **Abstract nouns** name a quality or a mental concept, something intangible that exists only in our mind. Examples of abstract nouns are beauty, courage, fun, and style.

## 1.3 Collective Nouns

A noun used to describe a group of people or things that is considered a single unit is called a **collective noun.** Some examples are

| | | |
|---|---|---|
| orchestra | family | band |
| herd | flock | chorus |
| committee | audience | gang |
| faculty | crowd | multitude |
| crew | staff | personnel |
| government | team | group |
| class | press | bunch |
| majority | nation | jury |

## 1.4 Countable and Noncountable Nouns

Most nouns can be made plural by changing the ending (usually by adding "s"), These are called **countable nouns.** There is a group of nouns, however, that have no plural. These are called **noncountable nouns,** because the members of the group they represent are either singular or plural depending on the context. Two main groups of noncountable nouns are mass nouns and abstract nouns.

### 1.4.1 Mass Nouns

| | | |
|---|---|---|
| cheese | moss | coffee |
| dust | wine | measles |

These are nouns that describe concrete objects considered in a mass quantity.

Occasionally, some of these nouns take a plural form if a variance of the object described is stressed.

How many *cheeses* (different kinds) did you taste?

That store carries more *teas* (kinds of) than any I've seen.

## Problem Solving Example:

Identify which of the following words are countable or noncountable by writing *countable* or *noncountable* in the blank provided.

a. _____ furniture

b. _____ dust

c. _____ penny

d. _____ virtue

e. _____ pizza

f. _____ coffee

a. *Furniture* is a noncountable noun.

b. *Dust* is a noncountable noun.

c. *Penny* is a countable noun.

d. *Virtue* is a countable noun.

e. *Pizza* is a countable noun.

f. *Coffee* is a noncountable noun.

## 1.5 Noun Compounds

A **compound** is a group of words (usually two) that functions as a single part of speech.

Her *mother-in-law* watched closely as the *blackbirds* fluttered about the *birdbath* behind the *flower garden*.

That *store clerk* had no *common sense*; he took the *traveler's check* without even checking the signature on a *credit card*.

**Noun compounds** generally take one of the following forms:

### *Noun and Noun*

|  |  |
|---|---|
| birdbath | credit card |
| bookstore | houseboat |

### *Adjective and Noun*

|  |  |
|---|---|
| blackbird | common sense |

### *Possessive Noun and Noun*

|  |  |
|---|---|
| traveler's check | citizens' committee |

### *Noun and Prepositional Phrase*

|  |  |
|---|---|
| mother-in-law | editor-in-chief |

### *Noun, Conjunction, and Noun*

|  |  |
|---|---|
| trial and error | breaking and entering |

### *Verb and Noun*

|  |  |
|---|---|
| search warrant | stoplight |

### *Gerund and Noun*

|  |  |
|---|---|
| firing squad | managing editor |

### *Noun and Verb*

|  |  |
|---|---|
| handclasp | ice skate |

### Preposition and Noun

downpour                    afterthought

### Noun and Gerund

problem solving             decision making

### Verb and Adverbial Preposition

break-in                    cleanup

## Problem Solving Example:

Identify the compound nouns in the following sentences.

a. Robert is the student who works in the Writing Lab.

b. Her grandfather's clock is a collector's item.

c. The students solved the problem by using common sense.

d. Today, students are frequently using credit cards to pay for a college education.

e. Bridget was a runner-up in the pageant.

f. In a recent meeting, the university's board of trustees gave the go-ahead to renovate the science building.

a. *Writing Lab* is a compound noun.

b. *Collector's item* is a compound noun.

c. *Common sense* is a compound noun.

d. *Credit card* is a compound noun.

e. *Runner-up* is a compound noun.

f. *Go-ahead* is a compound noun.

## 1.6    Gender

In English there are four genders. They are not indicated by inflective forms but by entirely different words.

| MASCULINE | FEMININE | COMMON *(either sex)* | NEUTER *(no sex)* |
|-----------|----------|-----------------------|-------------------|
| father | mother | parent | marriage |

## 1.7  Number—Plural Nouns

Most nouns can be singular or plural. The usual plural form adds –*s* to the end of the word.

| desk | desks | book | books |
|------|-------|------|-------|

However, there are exceptions to this guideline. After a –*y* preceded by a consonant, the –*y* changes to –*i* and –*es* is added.

| sky | skies | secretary | secretaries |
|-----|-------|-----------|-------------|

If the final –*y* is preceded by a vowel, no change is made, and the plural is formed by adding –*s*.

| decoy | decoys | attorney | attorneys |
|-------|--------|----------|-----------|

If the last sound in the word is –*s*, –*z*, –*ch*, –*sh*, or –*x*, then –*es* is added so that the word can be easily pronounced.

| class | classes | branch | branches |
|-------|---------|--------|----------|

However, if the –*ch* is pronounced –*k*, only –*s* is added.

| stomach | stomachs |
|---------|----------|

Often the final –*fe* or –*f* in one-syllable words becomes –*ves*.

| half | halves |
|------|--------|
| wife | wives |

There are exceptions, of course.

| chief | chiefs |
|-------|--------|
| roof | roofs |

Many nouns have plural forms that are irregular or the same.

| child | children | mouse | mice |
|-------|----------|-------|------|
| woman | women | series | series |

For nouns ending in "o," add "s" or "es" to form the plural. These spellings must be memorized individually.

> potato, potatoes      hero, heroes

Finally, there are a number of foreign words that have become part of the language and retain their foreign plural form. There is a trend to anglicize the spelling of some of these plural forms by adding "s" to the singular noun. In the list that follows, the letter(s) in parentheses indicate the second acceptable spelling as listed by Webster's *New Collegiate Dictionary.*

| | |
|---|---|
| datum | data |
| medium | media |
| crisis | crises |
| parenthesis | parentheses |
| criterion | criteria |
| phenomenon | phenomena (s) |

As you can see, there are many peculiarities associated with plural formation. It is advisable to have a dictionary on hand to check plural forms.

## Problem Solving Example:

 Correct any errors in noun plurals in the following sentences.

a. Two dormitorys are being renovated during summer break.

b. The remedial math instructor said, "Two halfs make a whole."

c. Dr. Shephard read the admission criterias to the incoming freshmen.

d. Mary bought a new pair of skies for the skiing trip.

e. I have three shelfs above my desk in my dorm room.

f. The childrens from the college's day care center will trick or treat through the halls of the Beam Administration Building on Halloween.

a.  *Dormitorys* is incorrect. The plural of *dormitory* is formed by changing the *y* to *i* and adding *es* (*dormitories*).

   b.  *Halfs* is incorrect. The plural of *half* is formed by changing the *f* to *v* and adding *es* (*halves*).

   c.  *Criterias* is incorrect. The plural of *criterion* is *criteria*.

   d.  *Skies* is incorrect. The plural of *ski* is formed by adding *s* (*skis*).

   e.  *Shelfs* is incorrect. The plural of *shelf* is formed by changing the *f* to *v* and adding *es* (*shelves*).

   f.  *Childrens* is incorrect. The plural of *child* is *children*. *Children* is an irregular plural form.

## 1.8 The Possessive Case

The possessive case of singular nouns and some singular indefinite pronouns is formed by adding an apostrophe and "s."

| | |
|---|---|
| a fox's cunning | the mother's hope |
| the girl's dress | anyone's choice |
| Mr. Smith's hopes | New Year's Day |

Also, add an apostrophe and "s" to singular nouns that end with an "s" or an "s" or a "z" sound, unless the sound is unpleasant or difficult to pronounce. Some writers use only the apostrophe for singular nouns that end with an "s" or an "s" or "z" sound.

The witness's testimony

Dickens's story OR Dickens' story

Unpleasant sound:

        Ulysses's travels     Moses's beliefs

The possessive case of plural nouns ending in "s" is formed by adding only an apostrophe.

| | |
|---|---|
| The foxes' cunning | the mothers' hope |
| the girls' dresses | the Roberts' address |

The possessive case of plural nouns not ending in "s" is formed by adding an apostrophe and an "s."

|  |  |
|---|---|
| the children's game | the men's story |
| the people's court | women's liberation |

**Errors to Avoid**

Do not use the possessive case of a noun when the plural form is needed.

| *NO* | *YES* |
|---|---|
| keeping up with the Joneses' | keeping up with the Joneses |
| the Kennedys' | the Kennedys |
| men's | men |

Some words, phrases, and expressions contain a fixed apostrophe:

for goodness' sake

bachelor's degree, bachelor's degrees

collector's item, collector's items

Sometimes the possessive case is not necessary:

|  |  |
|---|---|
| family support group | humanities scholar |
| teacher salaries | AIDS victims |

### 1.8.1 The "Of" Phrase

When the possessive form refers to an animate object, such as a person, the addition of apostrophe or apostrophe "s" to the noun is the standard procedure. However, an "of" phrase is more often preferred when the possession refers to an inanimate object. Therefore, we write:

| the color of the cup | *NOT* the cup's color |
|---|---|
| the lines of the paper | *NOT* the paper's lines |

Inanimate things do not possess. Unfortunately, this guideline has its own exceptions. There are many occasions when we use the possessive form to indicate possession for nouns referring to things.

The following are some exceptions:

**Expressions of time**

the year's end          a day's work

three weeks' pay          today's weather

*Nature*

the tree's roots          the moon's phases

*Money or Measure*

a dollar's worth          an arm's length

*Groups of People*

the newspaper's headlines          the restaurant's employees

There is no clear rule. Besides the idioms mentioned, there are numerous others that appear to violate even the most reliable rules.

the book's success          the policy's failure

The "of" phrase is sometimes used with nouns referring to animate objects, especially to modify a long or awkward construction and to avoid a piling up of possessives.

NO:    The dog's collar's latch was broken.

YES:    The latch of the dog's collar was broken.

Any name consisting of several words that would be awkward in the possessive also uses the "of" phrase.

NO:    The director of the Health, Education and Welfare Department's message to the president. . .

YES:    The message of the director of the Health, Education and Welfare Department to the president. . .

Always try to keep the reader or the listener in mind; use the construction that will convey your meaning most clearly.

## 1.8.2 Possessives in a Series

When one of the words in a series is a possessive, all of the other words in that series must also be in the possessive case.

NO: Bill, Henry, George, and my new restaurant . . .

YES: Bill's, Henry's, George's, and my new restaurant . . .

## Problem Solving Example:

Make the following sentences show a series possessive by rewriting the sentence.

a. Andy, Dick, and my papers were presented at the spring meeting of the American Chemical Society.

b. Ms. Smith, Mr. Hang, and my resumes will be posted on the Internet.

c. Bill, Henry, and my roommates are all from Trenton, New Jersey.

d. The nursing department, the dental hygiene department, and your department graduates all passed their licensing examinations, respectively.

a. *Andy, Dick* should be *Andy's, Dick's*. All words in a series must be possessive if one word is possessive (*my papers*).

b. *Ms. Smith, Mr. Hang* should be *Ms. Smith's, Mr. Hang's*. All words in a series must be possessive if one word is possessive (*my resumes*).

c. *Bill, Henry* should be *Bill's, Henry's*. All words in a series must be possessive if one word is possessive (*my roommates*).

d. *Nursing department, dental hygiene department* should be *nursing department's, dental hygiene department's*. All words in a series must be possessive if one word is possessive (*your department*).

### 1.8.3 Separate Possession in a Series

When each word in a series possesses something different, each noun takes its own possessive ending.

> NO:  James and Michael's paintings are similar.
>
> YES:  James' (or James's) and Michael's paintings are similar.
>
> NO:  The chef and chauffeur's uniforms continue to last.
>
> YES:  The chef's and chauffeur's uniforms continue to last.

## Problem Solving Example:

Revise the sentences below to show separate possession.

a. Professor Steed and Professor Luang are Juan and Sherrod history professors, respectively.

b. Tomorrow night, there are parties in Tameka and Grace dormitory rooms.

c. I am allowed to use both Mom and Dad computers.

d. Ty and Liza individual art is on display.

*a. Juan and Sherrod* should be *Juan's and Sherrod's* to show that Professor Steed is Juan's professor, and Professor Luang is Sherrod's professor.

b. *Tameka and Grace* should be *Tameka's and Grace's* to show they have different dormitory rooms.

c. *Mom and Dad* should be *Mom's and Dad's* to show they have separate computers.

d. *Ty and Liza* should be *Ty's and Liza's* to show that the art on display is the art they have produced separately from each other.

### 1.8.4 Joint Possession in a Series

When each word in a possessive series owns the same thing, the last noun takes the possessive ending.

NO: Let's go over to John's and Mary's house. (If you made "house" plural, you would be visiting two houses.)

YES: Let's go over to John and Mary's house.

## Problem Solving Example:

Revise the following sentences to show joint possession.

a. She is Juan and Sherrod history professor.

b. Tomorrow night, there is a party in Tameka and Grace dormitory room.

c. I am allowed to use Mom and Dad computer.

d. Ty and Liza collaborative art is on display.

a. *Juan* and *Sherrod* should be *Juan* and *Sherrod's* to show that Juan and Sherrod have the same professor.

b. *Tameka* and *Grace* should be *Tameka* and *Grace's* to show that Tameka and Grace share the same dormitory room.

c. *Mom* and *Dad* should be *Mom* and *Dad's* to show that Mom and Dad own the same computer.

d. *Ty* and *Liza* should be *Ty* and *Liza's* to show that the art on display is art they produced together.

### 1.8.5 Possession With Gerunds

A **gerund** looks like a verb but is used as a noun. It is the "ing" form of the verb. The participle looks like a gerund because it also ends in "ing," but it serves as an adjective, not as a noun. (See *Verbals* for further explanation of these terms.)

When a noun or a pronoun immediately precedes a gerund, it is usually possessive.

*His* arriving when he did pleased us all.

The *senators'* voting was divided.

However, if the word preceding the gerund is an inanimate object, we use the "of" phrase, because it is usually agreed that inanimate objects do not possess.

NO:    The car's starting delighted Susan.

YES:   The starting of the car delighted Susan.

## Problem Solving Example:

Identify correct possession with a gerund in the following sentences by writing correct or incorrect in the blank provided.

a.  _____ When they saw the burning of the building, they applauded.

b.  _____ The professors arguing was distracting.

c.  _____ The student shouting surprised the professor.

d.  _____ He thought nothing of the shampooing of the rug.

e.  _____ The mayor's announcing of a tax reduction surprised everyone.

a.  The sentence is correct because the inanimate object *building* should not be made possessive preceding the gerund *burning*.

b.  The sentence is incorrect because the noun *professors* preceding the gerund *arguing* should be made plural possessive (*professors'*).

c.  The sentence is incorrect because the noun *student* preceding the gerund *shouting* should be made singular possessive (*student's*).

d.  The sentence is correct because the inanimate object *rug* should not be made possessive preceding the gerund *shampooing*.

e.  The sentence is correct because the noun *mayor* preceding the gerund *announcing* should be made singular possessive (*mayor's*).

### 1.8.6   Parallel Possession

In parallel structure, parallel ideas are expressed in the same grammatical form. Therefore, in parallel construction, the possessive form is carried through.

    NO:   His life is more burdensome than his wife.

    YES:  His life is more burdensome than his wife's.

## Problem Solving Example:

 Make the following sentences show parallel possession.

   a. Your newspaper writer's work differs from my magazine writer.

   b. His work is better than his sister.

   c. As a mother, I find my role is similar to my teacher: I must be a role model.

   d. His career goal is different from her brother, who wants to become a pilot.

 a. *Your newspaper writer's* and *my magazine writer* must be made parallel. *My magazine writer* can be made parallel by adding an apostrophe and –*s* (*my magazine writer's*).

   b. The possessive *his* and *sister* must be made parallel. *Sister* can be made parallel by adding an apostrophe and –*s* (*sister's*).

   c. The possessive forms *my* and *teacher* must be made parallel. *Teacher* can be made parallel by adding an apostrophe and –*s* (*teacher's*).

   d. The possessive *his* and *brother* must be made parallel. *Her brother* can be made parallel by adding an apostrophe and –*s* (*brother's*).

### 1.8.7 Possessive Followed by an Appositive

When a possessive is followed by an **appositive** (a word or group of words complementing or supplementing another), apostrophe "s" is added to the appositive.

It was Jason, the gardener's, move.

An appositive (or explanatory word or group of words) set off by commas implies that it is not essential to the meaning of the sentence. In such a case, the possessive may be formed on both the main noun and the explanatory word or on only the explanatory word.

It was Jason's, the gardener's, move.

*or*

It was Jason, the gardener's, move.

## Problem Solving Example:

Rewrite the following sentences containing a possessive followed by an appositive in two ways. In sentence 1, make both the main noun and the explanatory word possessive. In sentence 2, make only the explanatory word possessive.

   a. We went to Joe, my friend, house for a party.

     1.

     2.

   b. Grape is Ann Wang, the professor of English, favorite flavor.

     1.

     2.

   c. What is John, the hairdresser, advice?

     1.

     2.

   d. Rochelle Hall, the largest dormitory, fire alarm sounded at midnight.

     1.

     2.

a. 1. We went to Joe's, my friend's, house for a party. The possessive is formed on both the main noun (*Joe's*) and the explanatory word (*friend's*).

2. We went to Joe, my friend's, house for a party.

   The possessive is formed only on the explanatory word (*friend's*).

b. 1. Grape is Ann Wang's, the professor of English's, favorite flavor.

   The possessive is formed on both the main noun (*Ann Wang's*) and the explanatory word (*English's*).

2. Grape is Ann Wang, the professor of English's, favorite flavor.

   The possessive is formed only on the explanatory word (*English*).

c. 1. What is John's, the hairdresser's, advice?

   The possessive can be formed on both the main noun (*John's*) and the explanatory word (*hairdresser's*).

2. What is John, the hairdresser's advice?

   The possessive is formed only on the explanatory word (*hairdresser*).

d. 1. Rochelle Hall's, the largest dormitory's, fire alarm sounded at midnight.

   The possessive is formed on both the main noun (*Rochelle Hall's*) and the explanatory word (*dormitory's*).

2. Rochelle Hall, the largest dormitory's, fire alarm sounded at midnight.
   The possessive is formed only on the explanatory word (*dormitory*).

## 1.8.8 Possession With Compound Words

Use the last word in a compound word to form the possessive, even if the compound is not hyphenated.

| SINGULAR POSSESSIVE | PLURAL | PLURAL POSSESSIVE |
|---|---|---|
| mother-in-law's | mothers-in-law | mothers-in law's |
| commander in chief's | commanders in chief | commanders in chief's |

## Problem Solving Example:

Complete the following sentences by supplying the correct form of the word in parentheses.

a. The _____ (editor in chief) duties were demanding.

b. My _____ (mother-in-law) cake was delicious.

c. The _____ (Queen of England) jewels were kept in a safe in the tower.

d. Are both your _____ (sons-in-law) degrees in finance?

e. The _____ (commander in chief) speech called for troops to maintain peace in war-torn Bosnia.

f. Our _____ (chief executive officer) trip has been canceled.

a. *Editor in chief* is made possessive by adding an apostrophe and –*s* to *chief* (*editor in chief's*).

b. *Mother-in-law* is made possessive by adding an apostrophe and –*s* to *law* (*mother-in-law's*).

c. *Queen of England* is made possessive by adding an apostrophe and –*s* to *England* (*Queen of England's*).

d. *Sons-in-law* is made possessive by adding an apostrophe and –*s* to *law* (*sons-in-law's*).

e. *Commander in chief* is made possessive by adding an apostrophe and –*s* to *chief* (*commander in chief's*).

f. *Chief executive officer* is made possessive by adding an apostrophe and –*s* to *officer* (*chief executive officer's*).

### 1.8.9  Double Possessive

A double possessive, perfectly acceptable in English, uses both apostrophe "s" and an "of" form.

friends of Mary's          relatives of Mr. Green's

## Problem Solving Example:

Complete the following sentences by supplying the correct form of the words in parentheses.

a. Ten _____ (soldier) of the _____ (major) platoon honored his career.

b. The _____ (classmate) of _____ (Sam) were happy he returned to school after his accident.

c. All _____ (relative) of _____ (Mr. Green) attended the family reunion.

d. Several _____ (student) of the _____ (professor) complained about his delay in returning tests.

e. Two _____ (member) of the _____ (college) security office staff talked about campus crime at the recent Greek Council meeting.

a. The word *soldier* preceding *of* is plural (*soldiers*). The word following *of* is possessive (*major's*).

b. The word *classmate* preceding the *of* is plural (*classmates*). The word following *of* is possessive (*Sam's*).

c. The word (*relative*) preceding *of* is plural (*relatives*). The word following *of* is possessive (*Mr. Green's*).

d. The word (student) preceding *of* is plural (*students*). The word following *of* is possessive (*professor's*).

e. The word (*member*) preceding *of* is plural (*members*). The word following *of* is possessive (*college's*).

CHAPTER 2

# Pronouns

## 2.1 Types of Pronouns

**Pronouns** are the simple, everyday words used to refer to the people, places, or things that have already been mentioned, such as *him, she, me,* and *it,* or to indefinite people, places, things, or qualities, such as *who, where, this,* and *somebody.* Pronouns usually replace some noun and make an expression concise. There are only about 50 pronouns in the English language, and most of them are short words; however, they can be difficult to use correctly. One reason these words may be so difficult to use properly is their frequency of occurrence. Of the 25 most commonly used words in the English language, ten are pronouns. Perhaps it is due to their frequent usage that pronouns have acquired a variety of distinctive functions.

Although pronouns are used in different ways, they have two things in common. The first is their ability to stand alone, or "stand in" for nouns. The second is that they all have little specific meaning. Whatever meaning they have derives from the context in which they are found. Some pronouns that modify other words are also adjectives. This chapter will speak mainly of pronouns that stand alone—that take the place either of a definite noun or of an unknown or uncertain noun. Pronouns used as adjectives are discussed in the chapter *Adjectives and Adverbs.* Pronouns used as adjectives in examples in this chapter are marked (a).

*Whom* are *you* speaking to?

That is *my* (a.) hat *you* are holding in *your* (a.) hand.

Marsha *herself* told them *all* (a.) about *what* happened to *her* when *it* started to rain.

*Somebody* had to let the others know *that she* was not to blame.

*Who*, *what*, *where*, *when*, and *how* are the five words by *which you* can organize *this*.

*This* is a new kind of information for *me*, and *I* regret to *some* (a.) degree *that I* can't be more in touch with *them*.

All the italicized words in the preceding sentences are pronouns. Traditionally, pronouns are divided into six groups; each group has its own name, definition, and special functions. These categories are helpful in learning how to recognize the different kinds of pronouns and how to use them correctly, since they come in such a wide variety of forms.

### 2.1.1 Personal Pronouns

Because of their many forms, these can be troublesome words.

## CASE

| Number | Person | Subject | Object | Possessive | Possessive Adjective |
|--------|--------|---------|--------|------------|----------------------|
| Singular | First | *I* | *me* | *mine* | *my* |
| | Second | *you* | *you* | *yours* | *your* |
| | Third* | | | | |
| | (masc.) | *he* | *him* | *his* | *his* |
| | (fem.) | *she* | *her* | *hers* | *her* |
| | (neuter) | *it* | *it* | | *its* |
| Plural | First | *we* | *us* | *ours* | *our* |
| | Second | *you* | *you* | *yours* | *your* |
| | Third | *they* | *them* | *theirs* | *their* |

Subject: _____ saw it. Object: Let _____ . Possessive: *That's* _____ .
Possessive Adjective: _____ house.

*When a pronoun is used to refer to someone (other than the speaker or the person spoken to), the third person is used, and a different form of the pronoun is employed to show the gender of the person referred to. *His*, *her*, *him*, *his* and *hers* all indicate the masculine or feminine gender. *It* and *its* refer to something to which gender does not apply.

There are three forms of personal pronouns as follows.

*PERSON:* to indicate whether the person is the speaker (first person), the person being spoken to (second person), or the person being spoken about (third person).

*CASE:* to show the job the pronoun is performing in the sentence.

*NUMBER:* to indicate whether the word is plural or singular.

### Examples of Personal Pronoun Use

*I* went yesterday to see *her.*

Between *you* and *me, I* really don't want to go with *him.*

### Errors to Avoid—Pronoun Case

When a compound subject or object includes a pronoun, be sure that the case chosen is in agreement with the pronoun's place and function in the sentence: a subject case pronoun is used as the subject of the verb, an object case pronoun is used as the object, etc. The same rule of agreement is true when using an appositive (a word or words with the same meaning as the pronoun); the pronoun must be in the same case form as the word it renames.

## Compounds

Both Mary and he (NOT him) have seen that movie.

(subject—"Mary and he")

Last year the team elected both Jane and me (NOT I).
(object—"Jane and me")

Could you wait for my brother and me (NOT I)?
(object of preposition—"my brother and me")

It was I (NOT me) who received the award.
(subject complement—"I")

## Appositions

We (NOT us) Americans value freedom. (*subject*)

Let's you and me (NOT I) go together. (*object*)

Our school sent two delegates, Mark and him (NOT he). (*object*)

It is not for us (NOT we) writers to determine editorial policy.
(*object*)

## Problem Solving Example:

Underline the correct pronoun in parentheses.

a. Between you and (I, me), I really do not want to date him.

b. Ms. Martinez and (I, me) will direct the chorus.

c. Let's you and (I, me) go to the lecture on panic disorder tonight.

d. (We, Us) students decided to purchase a personal computer from Best Buy.

e. It was (he, him) who left his chemistry notes in the library.

f. The vice president for academic affairs listened to the proposal written by Makita and (I, me).

a. *Me* is the correct answer. *Between* is a preposition and takes an object pronoun (*me*). *I* is incorrect because *I* is a subject pronoun.

b. *I* is the correct answer. *I* is a subject pronoun. The subject of the sentence is *Ms. Martinez* and *I*. *Me* is incorrect because *me* is an object pronoun.

c. *Me* is correct. *Me* is an object pronoun. *Me* is the appositive for the object of the verb *let* (*us*). *I* is incorrect because *I* is a subject pronoun.

d. *We* is the correct answer. *We* is a subject pronoun in apposition to *students*. *We students* is the subject of the sentence. *Us* is incorrect because *us* is an object pronoun.

e. *He* is the correct answer. *He* is a subject pronoun. It is the subject complement of the sentence. *Him* is incorrect because *him* is an object pronoun.

f. *Me* is the correct answer. *Me* is an object pronoun. It is the object of the preposition *by*.

## 2.1.2 Relative Pronouns—Interior Sentences (Clauses)

Relative pronouns play the part of subject or object in sentences within sentences (clauses). They often refer to nouns that have preceded them, making the sentence more compact.

> NO: The flower—the flower was yellow—made her smile.
>
> YES: The flower, *which* was yellow, made her smile.
>
> NO: The girl—the girl lived down the block—loved him.
>
> YES: The girl *who* lived down the block loved him.

Sometimes their reference is indefinite.

I wonder *what* happened. (The event that occurred is uncertain.)

I'll call *whomever* you want. (The people to be called are unknown.)

*Who* (for persons), *that* (for persons and things), *where* (for places, usually geographic), and *which* (for things and places) are the most common pronouns of this type.

## Problem Solving Example:

Underline the correct relative pronoun in parentheses.

a. Professor Woofruff is the one (who, which) assigned the take-home test.

b. The chemistry lab is the room (where, which) the microbiology study group will meet.

c. The instructor asked her students to purchase two books (who, which) are not listed on the course syllabus.

d. The computer lab (where, which) is located in Higgins Hall is open until midnight.

e. I cannot remember the fraternity (who, which) sponsored the party last night.

a. *Who* is the correct answer. *Who* refers to the *one* (a specific thing). *Which* is incorrect because *which* refers to things.

b. *Where* is the correct answer. *Where* refers to a place (a place that is known: the meeting place of the microbiology study group). *Which* is incorrect because *which*, although it refers to things and places, would need to be accompanied by the preposition *in* (*in which*) in this sentence.

c. *Which* is the correct answer. *Which* refers to *books*. *Who* is incorrect because *who* refers to a·person.

d. *Which* is the correct answer. *Which* refers to a place (computer lab). *Where* is incorrect because *where* cannot be the subject of the clause *which is located in Higgins Hall.*

e. *Which* is the correct answer. *Which* refers to the *fraternity*. *Who* is incorrect because it refers to a person.

### 2.1.3  Interrogative Pronouns—Questions

These pronouns are easy to recognize because they always introduce either direct or indirect questions. The words just discussed as relative pronouns are called interrogative pronouns when they introduce a question: *who, what, which, whom, whose, where, whoever, whichever,* and *whatever.*

*Who* is at the door? (refers to a person)

*What* do you want from me? (refers to a thing)

*Which* (flavor) do you want? (refers to a thing)

*Which* (boy) won the match? (refers to a person)

*Whatever* you mean by "liberal education," I don't know.

*Whom* did you telephone last night?

*Where* are you going?

Sometimes these relative pronouns introduce subordinate (dependent) clauses.

She wondered *who* was at the door.

Samuel asked them *what* they wanted.

He didn't know if he would ever find out *what* happened.

I couldn't guess *which* they would choose.

## Problem Solving Example:

 Using the following list of interrogative pronouns, complete the following sentences.

| who | whom | whoever |
|-----|------|---------|
| what | whose | whichever |
| which | | |

a. _____ of these different kinds of music is your favorite?

b. _____ calculus textbook is on the floor?

c. _____ can the Office of Career Development do for you?

d. _____ did the dean intend when he said that all freshmen must live on campus?

e. _____ will the graduation speaker be?

a. *Which* is the correct answer. *Which* refers to a thing (music).

b. *Whose* is the correct answer. *Whose* is a possessive pronoun referring to the owner of the calculus textbook. (*Which* is also an acceptable answer.)

c. *What* is the correct answer. *What* is used to introduce a question about a specific thing or place.

d. *Whatever* is the correct answer. *Whatever* refers to a thing (the dean's statement).

e. *Who* is the correct answer. *Who* refers to a person (graduation speaker).

## 2.1.4 Demonstrative Pronouns—Pointers

*This, that, these,* and *those* are the most common words used as pronouns to point to someone or something clearly expressed or implied.

*That* is the apple I wanted. (subject)

Bring me *those*, please. (object)

I must tell him *that*. (object)

*These* are the ones I've been looking for. (subject)

"*This* above all, to thine own self be true." (subject)

These same words are often used as adjectives, and at first glance it is easy to classify them only as adjectives, forgetting that they also take the place of nouns and serve as pronouns.

> *That* apple is the one I want. (adjective describing "apple")
> Bring me *those* books, please. (adjective describing "books")
> *Such* and *so* may also serve as pointing pronouns:
> *Such* was his fate. (subject)
> He resented Jerry and told him *so*. (object)

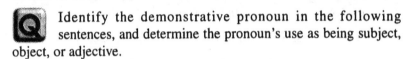

## Problem Solving Example:

Identify the demonstrative pronoun in the following sentences, and determine the pronoun's use as being subject, object, or adjective.

    a. That poetry book is the one I want to buy for my girlfriend's birthday present.

    b. My mother said, "Bring me those things."

    c. That is the best pizza I have ever eaten.

    d. These are the ones I have been looking for.

    e. My professor said, "Please pass this research paper to Emily."

**A**     a. *That* is a demonstrative pronoun used as an adjective to describe *book*.

    b. *Those* is a demonstrative pronoun used as an adjective to describe *things*.

    c. *That* is a demonstrative pronoun used as a subject.

    d. *These* is a demonstrative pronoun used as a subject.

    e. *This* is a demonstrative pronoun used as an adjective to describe *research paper*.

### 2.1.5 Reciprocal Pronouns

The reciprocal pronouns are *each other* and *one another*. Each other is preferred when the reference is two nouns, and *one another* is preferred when the reference is more than two nouns.

Romeo and Juliet love *each other*.

The members of the fraternity support *one another*.

### 2.1.6 Reflexive Pronouns

These are the pronouns that end in "self" or "selves."

| | | |
|---|---|---|
| myself | yourself | yourselves |
| himself | herself | itself |
| ourselves | themselves | |

Their main purpose is to reflect back on the subject of a sentence.

She cut *herself*. (object, refers to "she")

I bought *myself* a new dress. (indirect object, refers to "I" )

They consider *themselves* lucky. (object, refers to "they")

## Problem Solving Example:

Complete the following sentences using a reflexive pronoun from the list below.

| | | |
|---|---|---|
| myself | yourself | yourselves |
| himself | herself | itself |
| ourself | ourselves | |

a. We found _____ out of money.

b. I gave _____ a perm.

c. Give _____ the time needed.

d. The company declared _____ bankrupt.

e. They will give it to Tom _____ .

a. *Ourselves* is a reflexive pronoun that refers to the subject of the sentence *we*.

b. *Myself* is a reflexive pronoun that refers to the subject of the sentence *I*.

c. *Yourself* is a reflexive pronoun that refers to the understood subject of the sentence *you*.

d. *Itself* is a demonstrative pronoun that refers to the subject of the sentence *company*.

e. *Themselves* is a demonstrative pronoun that refers to the subject of the sentence *they*.

## 2.1.7 Intensive Pronouns

Reflexive pronouns also provide emphasis. When they serve this purpose, they are used to intensify the meaning of the noun or pronoun they accompany.

We will triumph over this outrage *ourselves*.

I will go to the ticket office *myself*.

She will tell it to him *herself*.

### Errors to Avoid—Reflexive Pronouns
Do not use the reflexive in place of the shorter personal pronoun.

NO:   Both Sandy and *myself* plan to go.

YES:   Both Sandy and *I* plan to go.

Watch out for careless use of the pronoun form.

NO:   George *hisself* told me it was true.

YES:   George *himself* told me it was true.

NO:   They washed the car *theirselves*.

YES:   They washed the car *themselves*.

Notice that the reflexive pronouns are not set off by commas.

NO:   Mary, *herself*, gave him the diploma.

YES:   Mary *herself* gave him the diploma.

## 2.1.8 Indefinite Pronouns

This group of pronouns acquired its name because the reference (the noun for which they are standing in) is indefinite.

### Indefinite persons or things (all singular pronouns)

| | |
|---|---|
| each | everything |
| either | something |
| one | anything |
| neither | nothing |
| everybody | everyone |
| somebody | someone |
| anybody | anyone |
| nobody | no one |
| other | |

*Everybody* joined in the chorus.

*No one* took less than he did.

Is *anyone* here?

I hope *someone* answers my calls.

### Indefinite quantities

| | | |
|---|---|---|
| one | neither | none |
| each | much | either |
| another | all | some |
| several | both | few |
| least | less | little |
| lots | many | plenty |
| other | most | more |

*Much* has been said on the subject of delinquency.

*Many* are called, but few are chosen.

*Each* must chart his own course.

The following pronouns are plural:

| | |
|---|---|
| several | both |
| few | many |

These pronouns may be singular or plural, depending on the use:

| | |
|---|---|
| all | none |
| some | any |
| most | more |

*Some* of the mail *has* arrived.

*Some* of the letters *have* arrived.

## 2.2 Case—The Function of the Pronoun in a Sentence

By far, the pronouns with which we are apt to make the most mistakes are those that change their form when they play different parts in a sentence—the personal pronouns and the relative pronoun *who*. A careful study of the peculiarities of these changes is necessary in order to avoid the mistakes associated with their use.

### 2.2.1 Subject Case (Used Mainly When the Pronoun is a Subject)

Use the *subject case* (*I, we, you, he, she, it, they, who,* and *whoever*) for the following purposes:

1.  As a subject or a repeated subject

    NO:     Mrs. Jones and *me* left early yesterday.

    YES:    Mrs. Jones and *I* left early yesterday. (subject of "left")

    NO:     I know *whom* that is.

    YES:    I know *who* that is. (subject complement of "is")

    NO:     *Us* girls always go out together.

    YES:    *We* girls always go out together. ("we" is the subject; "girls" repeats it)

2.  Following the verb "to be" when it has a subject

This is a part of the language that appears to be changing. It is a good example of how the grammar of a language follows speech and not the other way around. The traditional guideline has been that a pronoun following a form of "be" must be in the same case as the word before the verb.

It is *I*. ("It" is the subject; *I* is the subject complement.)

I thought it was *she*. ("It" is the subject; *she* is the subject complement.)

Was it *they* who arrived late? ("It" is the subject; *they* is the subject complement.)

Our ear tells us that in informal conversation, "It is I" would sound too formal, so instead we tend to say

It is *me*. (in conversation)

I thought it was *her*. (in conversation)

Was it *them* who arrived late? (in conversation)

In written English, however, it is best to follow the standard of using the subject case after the verb "be" when "be" is preceded by a word in the subject case, even though the pronoun is in the position of an object.

Here are some more examples that might cause trouble.

NO:     Last week the best students were *you* and *me*.

YES:    Last week, the best students were *you* and *I* (refers to "students," subject of "were")

NO:     Whenever I hear that knock, I know it must be *him*.

YES:    Whenever I hear that knock, I know it must be *he*. (refers to "it," subject of "must be")

3.    As a subject when the verb is omitted (often after *than* or *as*)

I have known her longer than *he*. ("has known her" is elliptical)

She sings as well as *I*. ("sing" is elliptical)

We do just as well in algebra as *they*. ("do" is elliptical)

He is much better than *I* at such calculations. ("than I am at such calculations"—"am" is elliptical)

To test whether the subject or the object form is correct, complete the phrase in your mind, and it will be obvious.

Often a relative pronoun like *that, which, who, whom,* or *whoever* will act as the subject of a clause.

Tell me *who* was singing.

Arnold knows something *that* was generally unknown.

Do you remember *which* is better?

Give it to *whoever* has the most need.

## Problem Solving Example:

Choose the correct pronoun in parentheses to complete the following sentences.

   a.  Both Peter and (I, me) went to the movies.

   b.  (He, him) and Troy met Susan at the college's spring picnic.

   c.  Professor Paden noticed that Joan and (her, she) left class early.

   d.  You and (I, me) have always understood each other.

   e.  (Us, We) students must be careful when walking across the campus after dark.

   f.  We sing just as well as (they, them).

   a.  *I* is the correct answer. *I* is a subject case pronoun. *I* is used to complete the compound subject of the sentence Peter and I. *Me* is incorrect because *me* is an object pronoun.

   b.  *He* is the correct answer. *He* is a subject case pronoun. *He* is part of the compound subject of the sentence. *Him* is incorrect because *him* is an object pronoun.

   c.  *She* is the correct answer. *She* is a subject case pronoun *She* is part of the nominative clause (*that Joan and she left class early*). *Joan and she* is the compound subject of that clause. *Her* is incorrect because *her* is an object pronoun.

   d.  *I* is the correct answer. *I* is a subject case pronoun. *I* is part of the compound subject of the sentence: *you and I. Me* is incorrect because *me* is an object pronoun.

e. *We* is the correct answer. *We* is a subject case pronoun. *We* is the subject of the sentence. The word *students* repeats *we*. *Us* is incorrect because *us* is an object pronoun.

f. *They* is a subject case pronoun. A subject case pronoun is used after *as* when the verb is omitted. *Them* is incorrect because *them* is an object pronoun.

## 2.2.2 Object Case (Used Mainly When the Pronoun is an Object)

Use the **object case** (*me, us, him, her, it, you, them, whom, whomever*) as follows:

1. As the direct or indirect object, object of a preposition, or repeated object

The postman gave *me* the letter. (indirect object)

Mr. Boone appointed *him* and *me* to clean the room. ("him and me" are the objects of "appointed" and the subject of the infinitive "to clean")

They told *us* managers to rewrite the first report. ("us" is the direct object of "told"; "managers" repeats *us*)

Between *you* and *me*, I'm voting Republican. (object of "between")

*Whom* were you thinking about? (object of "about")

2. As the subject of an infinitive verb

Janet invited *him* and *me* to attend the conference.

3. As an object when the verb or preposition is omitted

Father told my sister June more about it than (he told) *me*.

The telephone calls were more often for Marilyn than (they were for) *him*.

4. Following "to be"

In point number 2, it was shown that the subject of an infinitive verb form must be in the object case. The infinitive "to be" is an exception to this rule. Forms of "to be" must have the same case before and after the verb. If the word preceding the verb is in the subject case, the pronoun following must be in the subject case also (For example, It is *I*). If the word before the verb is an object, the pronoun following must be objective as well.

We thought the *author* of the note to be *her*.

You expected the *winner* to be *me*.

5.  Subject of a progressive verb form that functions as an adjective (participle—"ing" ending)

Two kinds of words commonly end in "ing": a *participle*, or a word that looks like a verb but acts like an adjective, and a *gerund*, a word that looks like a verb but acts like a noun. When an "ing" word acts like an adjective, its subject is in the object case.

Can you imagine *him acting* that way? ("Acting" refers to the pronoun and is therefore a participle, which takes a subject in the object case, "him.")

They watched *me smiling* at all the visitors. ("Smiling" refers to the pronoun, which must be objective, "me.")

### *Compare:*

Can you imagine *his acting* in that part? (Here the emphasis is on "acting"; "his" refers to "acting," which is functioning as a noun— it is a gerund—and takes the possessive case.)

It was *my smiling* that won the contest. (Emphasis is on "smiling"— it is playing the part of a noun and so takes a possessive case pronoun, "my.")

## Problem Solving Example:

 Choose the correct pronoun in parentheses to complete the following sentences.

a.  The talent committee selected (we, us) musicians to appear at the college's upcoming spring street carnival.

b.  The Newcomer's Award in Journalism is being presented to (her, she) and (I, me) at the honors ceremony tomorrow.

c. Our tour group missed the train because of Franz and (she, her).

d. The group asked (he, him) and (I, me) to drive to the beach.

e. Paul questioned (she, her) and (I, me) about the accident.

f. Our resident advisor told (we, us) girls to be quiet.

a. *Us* is the correct answer. *Us* is an object case pronoun. *Us* is the object of the verb *selected*. *We* is incorrect because *we* is a subject case pronoun.

b. *Her* and *me* are the correct answers. *Her* and *me* are object case pronouns. *Her* and *me* are objects of the preposition *to*. *She* and *I* are incorrect because *she* and *I* are subject case pronouns.

c. *Her* is the correct answer. *Her* is an object case pronoun. *Franz and her* is the object of the preposition *because of*. *She* is incorrect because *she* is a subject case pronoun.

d. *Him* and *me* are the correct answers. *Him* and *me* are object case pronouns. They are objects of the verb *asked*. *He* and *I* are incorrect because *he* and *I* are subject case pronouns.

e. *Her* and *me* are the correct answers. *Her* and *Me* are object case pronouns. The phrase *her and me* is the object of the verb *questioned*. *She* and *I* are incorrect because *she* and *I* are subject case pronouns.

f. *Us* is the correct answer. *Us* is an object case pronoun. *Us* is the object of the verb *told*. *We* is incorrect because *we* is a subject case pronoun.

### 2.2.3 Possessive Case

Use the **possessive adjective case** (*my, our, your, her, his, its, their, whose*) in the following situations:

1. To indicate possession, classification of something, or connection. Possession is the most common.

I borrowed *her* car. (The car belongs to her.)

Come over to *our* house. (The house belongs to us.)

The plant needs water; *its* leaves are fading.

2.  Preceding a verb acting as a noun (gerund)

*Our* leaving early helped end the party.

*Whose* testifying will you believe?

Since there are no possessive forms for the demonstrative pronouns *that*, *this*, *these*, and *those*, they do not change form before a gerund.

NO:    What are the chances of *that's* being painted today?

YES:    What are the chances of *that* being painted today?

Use the **possessive case** (*mine, ours, yours, hers, his, its, theirs, whose*) in any role a noun might play—a subject, an object, or a complement with a possessive meaning.

*Hers* was an exciting career. ("Hers" is the subject of "was.")

Can you tell me *whose* this is? ("Whose" is the complement of "is.")

He is a friend of *mine*. ("Mine" is the object of the preposition "of.")

We borrowed *theirs* last week; it is only right that they should use *ours* this week. ("Theirs" is the object of the verb "borrowed"; "ours" is the object of the verb "use.")

## Problem Solving Example:

Choose the correct form of the pronoun in parentheses to complete the following sentences.

a.  (Whose, Who) laptop computer is this?

b.  That dress in the closet is (her's, hers).

c.  (Her, She) arriving late angered Dr. Wood, who was in the middle of her lecture.

d.  The e-mail is (your's, yours).

e.  The cellular telephone needs recharging; (it's, its) batteries are low.

f.  (Their, Them) protesting got Dean Hanson's attention.

a.  *Whose* is the correct answer. *Whose* is a possessive case pronoun. *Whose* indicates possession of the laptop computer. *Who* is incorrect because *who* is a subject case pronoun.

b.  *Hers* is the correct answer. *Hers* is a possessive case pronoun. *Her* indicates possession of the dress. *Her's* is not a word.

c.  *Her* is the correct answer. In this sentence, *her* is used as a possessive case pronoun, which should precede the gerund *arriving*. *Him* is incorrect because *him* is an object case pronoun.

d.  *Yours* is the correct answer. The correct possessive form is *yours*. *Your's* is not a word.

e.  *Its* is the correct answer. *Its* is a possessive pronoun. *Its* indicates possession of the batteries (*cellular telephone*). *It's* is incorrect because it is the contraction for *it is*.

f.  *Their* is the correct answer. *Their* is a possessive case pronoun, which precedes the gerund *protesting*. *Them* is incorrect because *them* is an object case pronoun.

## 2.3   *Who* and *Whom*

*Who* is a subject case pronoun. It may be used as the subject or subject complement of an independent or a subordinate clause.

*Who* are you? (*Who* is the subject complement; it refers to the subject *you*.)

We were not sure *who her next opponent would be.* (In this subordinate clause, *who* is the subject complement referring to *opponent*, the subject of the clause.)

He is a person *who* we think *is very qualified for the position.* (In this subordinate clause, *who* is the subject of *is*.)

He is the person *who was selected for the job.* (In this subordinate clause, *who* is the subject of *was selected*.)

*Whom* is an object case pronoun. It may be used as a direct object, indirect object, or object of a preposition in an independent or a subordinate clause.

*Whom* would you like to speak to? (*Whom* is the object of the preposition *to*.)

*Whom* did you call? (*Whom* is the object of the transitive verb *did call*.)

We were not sure *for whom the bell tolled*. (In this subordinate clause, *whom* is the object of the preposition *for*.)

Voters elected a candidate *whom they could trust*. (In this subordinate clause, *whom* is the direct object of the transitive verb *could trust*.)

## Problem Solving Example:

Choose the correct form of the pronoun in parentheses.

a. (Who, Whom) is the winner of the Nobel Prize this year?

b. I must see the professor (who, whom) I spoke with last week.

c. Susan Williams is the candidate (who, whom) we believe is the best qualified to be the new president of Holman College.

d. John, (who, whom) played the lead in the play, received excellent reviews.

e. When will the college television station news anchors announce (who, whom) they believe won the election for student body president?

f. If you know (who, whom) sent the letter, please let me know.

a. *Who* is the correct answer. *Who* is a subject case pronoun. *Who* is a subject complement that refers to *winner*. *Whom* is incorrect because *whom* is an object case pronoun.

b. *Whom* is the correct answer. *Whom* is the object of the preposition *with* (with whom I spoke last week). *Who* is incorrect because *who* is a subject case pronoun.

c. *Who* is the correct answer. *Who* is the subject in the clause *who is best qualified . . . Whom* is incorrect because *whom* is an object case pronoun.

d. *Who* is the correct answer. *Who* is a subject case pronoun. *Who* is the subject of the subordinate clause *who played the lead in the school play. Whom* is incorrect because *whom* is an object case pronoun.

e. *Who* is the correct answer. *Who* is the subject of the clause *who won the election for the student body president. Whom* is incorrect because *whom* is an object case pronoun.

f. *Who* is the correct answer. *Who* is a subject case pronoun. *Who* is the subject of the subordinate clause *who sent the letter. Whom* is incorrect because *whom* is an object case pronoun.

## 2.4 *Whoever* and *Whomever*

*Whoever* is a subject case pronoun. It may be used as the subject or subject complement of a subordinate clause.

Give the ticket to *whoever wins.* (In this subordinate/noun clause, *whoever* is the subject of the verb *wins*; the entire clause is the object of the preposition *to*.)

Give the ticket to *whoever the winner is.* (In this subordinate/noun clause, *whoever* is the subject complement referring to *the winner*; the entire clause is the object of the preposition *to*.)

*Whomever* is an object case pronoun. It may be used as an object in a subordinate clause.

Give the ticket to *whomever the committee recommends.* (In this subordinate clause, *whomever* is the direct object of the transitive verb *recommends*; the entire clause is the object of the preposition *to*.)

## Problem Solving Example:

Choose the correct form of the pronoun in parentheses.

a. This book will go to (whoever, whomever) lost it.

b. The club is entitled to choose (whoever, whomever) it wants for president.

c. Give the job to (whomever, whoever) the hiring committee recommends.

d. Each year the chancellor's award is given to (whomever, whoever) has the highest grade point average.

a. *Whoever* is the correct answer. *Whoever* is a subject pronoun. *Whoever* is the subject of the subordinate clause *whoever lost it*. *Whomever* is incorrect because *whomever* is an object pronoun.

b. *Whomever* is the correct answer. *Whomever* is the object of the transitive verb *wants* in the subordinate clause *whomever it wants for president*. *Whoever* is incorrect because *whoever* is a subject pronoun.

c. *Whomever* is the correct answer. *Whomever* is the object of the transitive verb *recommends* of the subordinate clause *whomever the hiring committee recommends*. *Whoever* is incorrect because *whoever* is a subject pronoun.

d. *Whoever* is the correct answer. *Whoever* is a subject pronoun. *Whoever* is the subject of the subordinate clause *whoever has the highest grade point average*. *Whomever* is incorrect because *whomever* is an object pronoun.

## 2.5 Agreement

A pronoun usually takes the place of some noun. The noun (or group of words that works as a noun) for which the pronoun stands in is called the **antecedent**. It usually comes before the pronoun in the sentence or the paragraph. It is important to remember that the pronoun and the word(s) it refers to have to agree. If the antecedent is plural, the pronoun must be plural; if the antecedent is singular, the pronoun must also be. The gender and person must also be consistent.

The *woman* raised *her* hand.

The *children* raised *their* hands.

## Problem Solving Example:

Correct any errors in pronoun-antecedent agreement in the following sentences by writing the correction above the line. If the sentence contains no errors in pronoun-antecedent agreement, write Correct in the blank provided.

    a. _____Every resident in the women's dorm must keep their room clean.

    b. _____ The brothers rented a movie, and they enjoyed it.

    c. _____ Tim's hat gets blown away whenever it is not on his head tightly.

    d. _____ The jury did their job.

    e. _____ Each law school student has their review for the bar exam on Monday night.

    f. _____ Susan left her identification card in the library.

    a. Change *their* to *her*. The antecedent is the singular noun *every resident*.

    b. This sentence is correct. The antecedents for the pronouns *they* and *it* are *brothers* and *movie* respectively.

    c. This sentence is correct. The antecedent for *it* is *hat*.

    d. Change *their* to *its*. *Jury*, a collective noun, has a singular meaning in this sentence since the jury is acting as a unit.

    e. Change *their* to *his* or *his or her*. The antecedent for the pronoun *their* is *each law student*, which is singular.

    f. This sentence is correct. The antecedent for *her* is *Susan*.

## 2.5.1 Number

Number refers to whether a pronoun is singular or plural. A singular pronoun should be used with a singular antecedent:

*Every dog* has *its* day.

A plural pronoun should be used with a plural antecedent:

*All pet owners* must feed *their* pets.

## 2.5.2 Gender

Gender refers to whether a pronoun is masculine, feminine, or neuter.

The woman has *her* share of problems. (feminine)

The man has *his* share of problems. (masculine)

The country has *its* share of problems. (neuter)

# 2.6 Reference Pronouns

## 2.6.1 Ambiguous Pronouns

Can you make sense out of the following paragraph?

*Harry called to David while he was coming down the stairs. David told Harry that he should not talk for long since he had laryngitis. Harry said that it wouldn't take long. Then he told David that he had seen him raking leaves. He said that he made a big mistake. David asked what he had done wrong. Harry replied that everyone could see where he made his mistake that looked closely.*

Try it now.

*Harry was coming downstairs when he called out to David. David said, "I can't talk very long; I have laryngitis."*

*Harry replied, "This won't take long. I saw you when I was raking leaves, and I want to tell you that you made a big mistake."*

*David asked, "What did I do wrong?"*

*Harry replied, "Anyone who looked closely could see what you did wrong."*

Pronouns can add grace and variety to our writing. Yet they become a problem when we use them too much or when it is difficult to tell exactly what or whom the pronoun is referring to. This is the most important lesson to learn about pronouns: make sure that it is clear what the pronoun is referring to.

> NO:   It was dark and it was heavy, and I tripped over it and dropped it down the stairs.

> YES:   It was dark, and the box was heavy. I tripped over something and dropped the box down the stairs.

> NO:   When Mary saw Anne, she told her that she would be happy to help her with the project.

> YES:   When Mary saw Anne, Anne told her that she would be happy to help Mary with the project.

> NO:   He was late, but he didn't know it.

> YES:   He was late, but Andy didn't know it.

*Who* and *which* and *that* can create similar problems. Make sure that it is clear what each pronoun refers to.

> NO:   Tom said he saw a cute little monkey who usually doesn't care about animals.

> YES:   Tom, who usually doesn't care about animals, said he saw a cute little monkey.

> NO:   He charged so high a price for the job that is generally considered unethical.

> YES:   He charged so high a price for the job that it is generally considered unethical.

> NO:   My father is quite famous as a chemist, which I know nothing about.

> YES:   My father is quite famous as a chemist, but I know nothing about chemistry.

When readers see a pronoun, they look for a nearby noun to determine what the pronoun stands for. If the noun is too far away, readers have to hunt for it. This slows down and irritates readers.

NO: I shut the door and concentrated only on my work. It was old and heavy and shut out every sound.

YES: I had to concentrate on my work, so I shut my door. It's old and heavy, and it keeps out every sound.

## Problem Solving Example:

Determine if the pronoun reference is clear in the following sentences. If the reference is clear, write Correct in the blank provided. If the reference is unclear, write X in the blank provided.

a. _____ The professor asked me to write an extra paper, but I'm not interested in it.

b. _____ Jane and Betty were relieved when Betty's letter of acceptance from Smith College arrived.

c. _____ The dog chased the cat up the oak tree. I had to call the fire department to get it down.

d. _____ The computer lab has both MACs and PCs. I think MACs are easier to operate.

e. _____ The doctor told his patient that he had won the lottery.

a. This sentence is incorrect. There is no clear antecedent for the pronoun *it*. Change *it* to *writing another paper.*

b. This sentence is correct. The repetition of the proper noun *Betty* makes the meaning of this sentence clear to the reader.

c. This sentence is incorrect. The reader cannot determine from the sentence if the pronoun *it* refers to the *dog* or the *cat*. Change *it* to *the cat.*

d. This sentence is correct. The repetition of *MACs* makes the meaning of the sentence clear to the reader.

e. This sentence is incorrect. The reader cannot determine who won the lottery—the doctor or the patient. Change *he* to *he himself.*

## 2.6.2  Use of *That* and *Which*

The use of *that* and *which* often presents a problem for the writer. The difference is simple: If the clause is essential to the meaning of the sentence, use *that*. If the clause is not essential to the meaning of the sentence, use *which*, and set off the clause with commas.

THAT:  The book that contained the formula was missing. (*It is essential that the formula be in the missing book.*)

WHICH: The book, which contained the formula, was missing. (*It is essential only that the book is missing.*)

CHAPTER 3

# Expletives

## 3.1 It

Dictionaries say that *it* and *there* are pronouns, but actually they have another use that is somewhat different from that of pronouns. They have even less meaning than the sometimes vague or indefinite pronouns. Because they provide so little information, their sole function is to fill space and to provide a formal subject for a sentence.

### 3.1.1 *It*—Impersonal and *It*—Real Subject

When *it* introduces sentences about the weather, time, or date, it is the real subject. *It* is also the real subject when it substitutes for a noun.

*It*'s cold outside. (what is "it"?)

*It*'s March 3.

What is this? *It*'s my comb. (Real subject—pronoun)

It's ten after three.

*It*'s a twenty-minute walk to the grocery store.

*It* seems warmer than yesterday.

I know *it* gets crowded here at noon.

### 3.1.2 *It*—Anticipatory

Sometimes *it* fills the subject position, while the actual subject appears later in the sentence. In this usage, *it* is an expletive. The nonitalicized sections of the following sentences are the actual subjects, and *it* is used as an expletive in each sentence.

*It's surprising* how handsome he is.

*It's interesting* to know your background.

*It's curious* that Mary paints so well.

*It's good* knowing you are waiting for me.

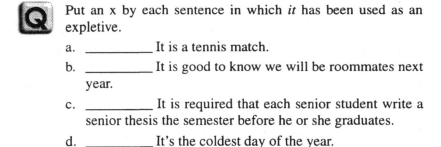

## Problem Solving Example:

Put an x by each sentence in which *it* has been used as an expletive.

a. _____ It is a tennis match.

b. _____ It is good to know we will be roommates next year.

c. _____ It is required that each senior student write a senior thesis the semester before he or she graduates.

d. _____ It's the coldest day of the year.

Sentences b and c use *it* as an expletive. In a and d *it* is the real subject of the sentence.

## 3.2   There

### 3.2.1   *There* as an Expletive

Notice how *there* has no meaning but only fills the space of the subject.

In these sentences, *there* is not the real subject; it is an expletive.

*There* are three of us watching you.

*There* is lightning outside.

*There* are many ways to peel an onion.

*There*'s a sale at Sears.

## Problem Solving Example:

Place an X by each sentence in which *there* is an expletive.

a. _____ There are only a few chances left.

b. _____ There are several ways to find a summer job.

c. _____ There is a new Italian restaurant opening today.

d. _____ There is good campus security at my college.

e. _____ There is the man who won the lottery.

All sentences except e use *there* as an expletive.

### 3.2.2  *There* as an Adverb

*There* is also often used as an adverb. If *there* is an expletive (a space filler), it is likely to be accompanied by "a." If it is accompanied by "the," it is probably an adverb and not a space filler.

*There* she is . . . Miss America.

*There* in the middle of the highway was a bag full of money.

*There* she goes.

*There* is the money on the table.

# CHAPTER 4

# Verbs

## 4.1 Kinds of Verbs

Every sentence must have a **verb**. Verbs express action or a state of being. Small changes in their form reflect many differences in meaning. One variable is number: a verb can be either singular or plural.

I *am* happy to be here. (singular)

We *are* not so sure of the date. (plural)

Jill *loves* chocolate chip cookies. (singular)

Mother and father *love* to go sailing. (plural)

Verbs are also distinguished by person: first (*I*, *we*), second (*you*), and third (*he*, *she*, *it*, *one*, *they*). Usually, verbs change form only in the third person singular.

I, you, we, they *hope* you will stay.

He, she *hopes* you will leave.

Changes made in the forms of words in order to indicate slight changes of meaning are called **inflections**. Verbs change more readily and more often than any other sort of word; this change can be confusing. By hearing English spoken and by learning to speak it yourself, you have probably learned the rules and peculiarities associated with correct verb usage without even thinking about it; you know that when something "sounds right," it probably is. But there are rules and logic to explain why some things sound right and others don't. When something sounds wrong to your ear, it is probably due to a mistake in either tense, irregular verb usage, or agreement.

## 4.1.1 Transitive Verbs and Objects

Verbs can express action. The subject is the one who does the action. The noun that receives the action is the **object**.

Harold studied *physics*.

Charles invited *Mary and David*.

This machine cleans *carpets*.

When a verb takes an object to complete its meaning, it is called a *transitive verb*. A transitive verb usually needs an object to make sense.

> NO: The company built.
>
> YES: The company built an alarm into the system.
>
> NO: Ellen and Harry thanked.
>
> YES: Ellen and Harry thanked their lucky stars.
>
> NO: We all make.
>
> YES: We all make our own breakfast.

Sometimes transitive verbs can be without an object, as in *Harold studied* or *This machine cleans*. However, they usually take an object.

A noun or pronoun is called the **direct object** when it is the direct receiver of the action of the verb, as in the examples above. The **indirect object** is the noun or pronoun that tells us *to whom* or *for whom* the action was done. The indirect object follows the verb and precedes the direct object. In the following examples, the italicized words are indirect objects.

Did they leave *us* any cake? (Did they leave any cake for us?)

Are you talking to *me*?

Alan bought *Susan* a racing bike. (Alan bought a racing bike for Susan.)

If the preposition *to* or *for* is present in the sentence, then the noun or pronoun for whom or to whom the action is done is the object of the preposition, not the indirect object.

Michael wrote a song for *Daphne*.

Did you give the key to *Jennifer*?

### 4.1.2 Intransitive Verbs and Complements

**Intransitive verbs** are verbs that do not take an object. They can stand alone with the subject.

The sun also *rises*.

Babies must *crawl* before they can *walk*.

Intransitive verbs often use complements to complete their meaning. Complements are quite different from objects. They do not receive the action of the verb, but they complete its meaning.

The sun rises *early*.

The baby can crawl *quite quickly*.

Notice that the complements in the above examples are an adverb or an adverbial (a word or group of words that acts like an adverb). Intransitive verbs use adverbs as complements. Copulative (linking) verbs can use adjectives as complements, but intransitive verbs cannot.

NO:   The baby can crawl so *quick*!

YES:  The baby can crawl so *quickly*!

NO:   He moved *cautious*.

YES:  He moved *cautiously*.

## Problem Solving Example:

Identify the direct object and indirect object in the following sentences.

a. My sisters gave our mother a day at the spa for Mother's Day.

b. Samantha bought her parents a farm in the mountains.

c. Cindy asked her brother a question about the recent stress management lecture.

   d. Samuel told Hannah the computer lab hours.

   e. Teresa gave Craig a surprise birthday party.

   a. *Day* is the direct object. The direct object receives the action of the verb *gave*. *Mother* is the indirect object. The indirect object tells to whom or for whom the action was (My sisters gave a day at the spa to mother).

   b. *Farm* is the direct object. The direct object receives the action of the verb *bought*. *Parents* is the indirect object. The indirect object tells to whom or for whom the action was done. (Samantha bought a farm for her parents.)

   c. *Question* is the direct object. The direct object receives the action of the verb *asked*. *Brother* is the indirect object. The indirect object tells to whom or for whom the action was done. (Cindy asked a question to her brother.)

   d. *Hours* is the direct object. The direct object receives the action of the verb *told*. *Hannah* is the indirect object. The indirect object tells to whom or for whom the action was done. (Samuel told the computer lab hours to Hannah.)

   e. *Birthday party* is the direct object. The direct object receives the action of the verb (*gave*). *Craig* is the indirect object. The indirect object tells to whom or for whom the action was done. (Teresa gave a surprise birthday party to Craig.)

## Problem Solving Example:

Determine if the following sentences contain a transitive or intransitive verb.

   a. Charles told Maria and Darrell of a party at the Mills Student Union.

   b. Dennis cried to his girlfriend about his low economics grade.

   c. My communications professor always says, "Think before you speak."

d.  Wang showed Sung the new computer printer.

e.  At 3:00 p.m. each day, the bell rings to end school.

a.  *Told* is a transitive verb. A transitive verb takes an object (*Maria and Darrell*).

b.  *Cried* is an intransitive verb. *Dennis* is the subject. *Cried* is the verb. *Dennis cried* can stand alone as a sentence.

c.  *Think* is an intransitive verb. In this command, *you* is the understood subject. The command *You think* can stand alone as a sentence. *Says*, the verb in the sentence introducing the quotation, is transitive.

d.  *Showed* is a transitive verb. A transitive verb takes an object (*printer*).

e.  *Rings* is an intransitive verb. *Bell* is the subject. *Rings* is the verb. *The bell rings* can stand alone as a sentence.

### 4.1.3 Copulative or Linking Verbs and Complements— Sensing Verbs

A verb describes either an action or a state of being. Transitive and intransitive verbs describe actions. **Copulative verbs** describe only states of being. The verb *to be* is the most common copulative verb. Others are *act, appear, seem, become, remain, look, sound, feel, smell, taste*, and *grow*.

The complement of a copulative verb refers to the subject. It modifies or completes the meaning of the subject.

The complement of a copulative verb may be a noun:

Ben Jonson was a *contemporary* of Shakespeare.

*Moby-Dick* is a complex *book*.

a nominal (a word or group of words that acts like a noun):

His argument was *that man is a rational creature*.

or an adjective:

His head feels *cool*.

Copulative verbs always take an adjective for a complement rather than an adverb. This usage may sometimes sound funny, but it makes better sense.

**Compare:**

| *Sensing Verb* | *Intransitive Verb* |
| --- | --- |
| The radiator felt cool. | Ralph behaved coolly. |
| Some fruits are quite bitter. | A spoiled child was crying bitterly. |

Linking verbs occasionally take adverbials as complements, particularly adverbials of time or place.

The professor is *in his office.*

The plane is *on the runway.*

**Linking Verbs:**

| | | |
| --- | --- | --- |
| be | shall be | should be |
| being | will be | would be |
| am | has been | can be |
| is | have been | could be |
| are | had been | should have been |
| was | shall have been | would have been |
| were | will have been | could have been |

**Verbs of the Senses:**

| | | | |
| --- | --- | --- | --- |
| appear | grow | seem | stay |
| become | look | smell | taste |
| feel | remain | sound | turn |

## Problem Solving Example:

Underline the linking verb in the following sentences.

a.  These pears taste delicious.

b. Sarah was my roommate during my sophomore year at Brevard College.

c. He should be department chairperson.

d. The cafeteria food smells terrible.

e. I am a finalist for a Morehead Scholarship.

a. *Taste* is a linking verb that refers to the sense of taste. *Delicious* is a complement that describes the subject *pear*.

b. *Was* is a linking verb. *Was* is a form of the verb *to be*. *Roommate* is the complement.

c. *Should be* is a linking verb. *Should* is the auxiliary/helping verb; *be* is the linking verb. *Department chairperson* is a complement that refers to the subject *He*.

d. *Smells* is the linking verb that refers to the sense of smell. *Terrible* is a complement that describes the subject *food*.

e. *Am* is a linking verb. *Finalist* is a complement that refers to the subject *I*.

### 4.1.4 Auxiliaries

| | | |
|---|---|---|
| has | can | might |
| have | may | must |
| had | should | do |
| shall | would | will |
| did | could | does |
| is | | |

All forms of the verb *be* are auxiliaries when they accompany a main verb, for instance, *is leaving* and *was going*.

## Problem Solving Example:

Identify the verbs in the following sentences by underlining the auxiliary verb once and the main verb twice.

a. Joe is going to graduate school at the University of Pennsylvania this fall.

b. Will Sally take the GRE this April?

c. He should go to the doctor.

d. Do you remember your first day in college?

e. She has been playing the piano since age seven.

f. Tomisha will attend Clemson University next year.

a. *Is going* is the verb. *Is* is the auxiliary verb. *Going* is the main verb.

b. *Will* is the auxiliary verb. *Take* is the main verb. The subject *Sally* comes between the auxiliary verb and the main verb. The sentence may be rewritten *Sally will take the GRE in April.*

c. *Should go* is the verb. *Should* is the auxiliary verb. *Go* is the main verb.

d. *Do* is the auxiliary verb. *Remember* is the main verb. The sentence may be rewritten *You do remember your first day in college.*

e. *Has been playing* is the verb. *Has* and *been* are auxiliary verbs. *Playing* is the main verb.

f. *Will attend* is the verb. *Will* is the auxiliary verb. *Attend* is the main verb.

## 4.2   Forms of English Verbs

With the exception of *be* which has eight forms, every English verb, whether regular or irregular, has five forms:

|  | *REGULAR* | *IRREGULAR* |
|---|---|---|
| the base form | walk | go |
| the –s form | walks | goes |
| the –ing (present participle) form | walking | going |

| | | |
|---|---|---|
| the *–ed* past form | walked | went |
| the past participle form | walked | gone |

## 4.3  Tense

**Tense** relates to time. Verbs have the ability to tell us not only what action is occurring but also when it is occurring. The form of a verb changes in order to indicate when an action takes place. The two main forms of any verb are the present and the past tense. The past tense is usually formed by adding *–ed* to the basic verb.

| *PRESENT* | *PAST* |
|---|---|
| walk | walked |
| listen | listened |
| enter | entered |

Verbs that follow this pattern in forming the past tense are called regular verbs. Almost all of the verbs in the language are regular. Yet, there are about 100 commonly used verbs that do not follow this pattern. These are known as irregular verbs and will be discussed in more detail later in the chapter.

Although the past and present are the only form changes in single-word verbs, there are certain verb phrases that are also used with the verbs to indicate changes in time. When these verb phrases are added to the past and present tenses, there are actually six tenses in the English language.

| | |
|---|---|
| *Present:* | present time, action or condition going on now (*yawn, am yawning*). |
| *Past:* | past time, action is completed (*yawned*). |
| *Future:* | future time, action or condition is expected to happen or come (*will yawn, shall yawn*). |
| *Present Perfect:* | action occurred in the past and is completed in the present (*have* or *has yawned*). |
| *Past Perfect:* | past action completed before another past action (*had yawned*). |

*Future Perfect:*   future action to be completed before another future action (*will have yawned*).

As you can see, some of these tenses make it possible to express quite subtle variations in time. The three perfect tenses as well as the future tense are formed by adding a helping, or auxiliary, verb to the past participle, which is usually formed by adding *–ed* to the main verb. The perfect tenses show that an action has been completed (perfected).

All six of the main tenses also have a companion form: the progressive form. This can also be considered a tense, as it shows that action is in progress. Progressive forms are expressed with some form of the verb *to be* and the ending *–ing* added to the main verb.

Examples:

He *is looking at* the birds. (present progressive)

They *were looking* at the mirror. (past progressive)

He *will be looking* for her tomorrow. (future progressive)

I *have been looking* at the tree. (present perfect progressive)

We *had been looking* for a house. (past perfect progressive)

She *will have been looking* for the right material for her drapes for three years. (future perfect progressive)

It is not necessary to learn the names of all these tenses; they are introduced only so that you may gain some familiarity with the terms and a better understanding of the logic behind the language. The most important parts of the study of verb forms for an English-speaking student are both the study of common errors and practice in using the correct forms.

The verbs that are apt to cause the most trouble are the irregular verbs, because it is easy to confuse the past tense and the past participle.

He drank (NOT drunk) his fill of beer.

After he had eaten (NOT ate) his dinner, he left.

I had gone (NOT went) down to see Jim.

He began (NOT begun) his day early.

To review, the regular verbs form the past tense by adding "d" or "ed" to the present tense of the verb. The irregular verbs form the past tense in a number of different ways; there are no rules governing the formation of the past tense and the past participles. They have to be studied and learned. Review this list of commonly used irregular verbs in section 4.4.1 to find the ones that most often cause you trouble.

### Errors to Avoid in Tense of Verbs

Do not use the present for the past tense.

NO: Yesterday, he *sees* her twice.

YES: Yesterday, he *saw* her twice.

Do not use the present for the future tense.

NO: Tomorrow I *drive* into town.

YES: Tomorrow I *shall drive* into town.

Do not use the past tense for factual information about literature.

NO: My teacher explained that *all right was* two words.

YES: My teacher explained that *all right is* two words.

Do not use the past for the past perfect tense.

NO: John asked whether I *ate* all my dinner.

YES: John asked whether I *had eaten* all my dinner.

Do not shift from the present to the past in the same phrase.

NO: The boy *is raking* the leaves and *went* for the basket.

YES: The boy *is raking* the leaves and *goes* for the basket.

Do not shift from the past to the present in the same phrase.

NO: She *sat* at the window and *looks* out.

YES: She *sat* at the window and *looked* out.

## Problem Solving Example:

Complete the following sentences by using the verb and the tense shown in parentheses.

a. We _____ (leave, future perfect) for class by the time you read this note.

b. My roommate _____ (talk, past tense) all night about her upcoming statistics test.

c. Henny _____ (walk, future tense) alone to the library after dark.

d. Richard and Henry _____ (plan, past progressive) a trip to Virginia Beach.

e. I _____ (accept, present perfect) a job at IBM.

f. My son Charles _____ (look, future progressive) for a summer job.

a. *Will have left* is the future perfect tense. The future perfect tense is made up of *will* + *have/has* + past participle. The auxiliary verb *will* points toward the future. The auxiliary verb *have* is needed for the perfect tense. The verb *leave* is an irregular verb. *Leave* changes to *left* in the past participle. The past participle is needed for the perfect tense. The future perfect tense shows one future action will happen before another future action. (The leaving for class will occur before the finding of the note.)

b. The past tense is formed by adding *–ed* to the base form of the regular verb. The past tense of the regular verb *talk* is *talked*. The past tense shows an action was completed at an earlier time. (The roommate's talking all night came before the beginning of the next day.)

c. *Will walk* is the future tense. The future tense is made up of the auxiliary verb *will* + base verb. The auxiliary verb *will* points to the future. The future tense shows an action is expected to happen at a future time. (Henny will go to the library at a future time: after dark).

d. *Were planning* is the past progressive tense. The past progressive tense is made up of the past tense auxiliary verb *be (was/were)* + *–ing* added to the base form of the verb. The auxiliary verb *were* is the past tense of the verb *be*. *Planning* is made up of *–ing* added to base verb *plan*. The past progressive tense shows an action was in process at a certain time in the past. (Richard and William were in the process of planning their trip at a certain time in the past.)

e. *Have accepted* is the present perfect tense. The present perfect tense is made up of the present tense form (*have/has*) of the auxiliary verb *have* + the past participle of the base form of the verb. The past participle is made by adding *–ed* to the base form of the regular verb *accept (accepted)*. The present perfect tense shows an action occurred in the past and is completed in the present. (The person accepted the position in the past, but the person begins the position in the present.)

f. *Will be looking* is the future progressive tense. The future progressive tense is made up of the auxiliary verb *will* + a form of the verb *be* + the *–ing* form of the base verb. The auxiliary verb *will* points to the future. The future progressive tense shows an action that is in progress at a future time. (Charles is in the process of looking for a summer job at a future time.)

## 4.4 Regular and Irregular Verbs

### 4.4.1 Main Parts of Commonly Used Irregular Verbs

| PRESENT TENSE | PAST TENSE | PAST PARTICIPLE |
|---|---|---|
| am | was | been |
| arise | arose | arisen |
| awake | awoke, awaked | awaked, awoken |
| bear | bore | borne |

| PRESENT TENSE | PAST TENSE | PAST PARTICIPLE |
|---|---|---|
| beat | beat | beaten |
| become | became | become |
| begin | began | begun |
| bend | bent | bent |
| bind | bound | bound |
| bite | bit | bitten |
| bleed | bled | bled |
| blow | blew | blown |
| break | broke | broken |
| bring | brought | brought |
| broadcast | broadcast, broadcasted | broadcast, broadcasted |
| build | built | built |
| burn | burned, burnt | burned, burnt |
| burst | burst | burst |
| buy | bought | bought |
| cast | cast | cast |
| choose | chose | chosen |
| cling | clung | clung |
| come | came | come |
| cost | cost | cost |
| creep | crept | crept |
| deal | dealt | dealt |
| dig | dug | dug |
| dive | dived, dove | dived |
| do | did | done |
| *drag | dragged | dragged |

*Not an irregular verb, but past forms are often misused (*drug* for the past form of *drag,* for instance).

| PRESENT TENSE | PAST TENSE | PAST PARTICIPLE |
|---|---|---|
| draw | drew | drawn |
| dream | dreamed, dreamt | dreamed, dreamt |
| drink | drank | drunk |
| drive | drove | driven |
| *drown | drowned | drowned |
| eat | ate | eaten |
| fall | fell | fallen |
| feed | fed | fed |
| fight | fought | fought |
| find | found | found |
| flee | fled | fled |
| fling | flung | flung |
| *flow | flowed | flowed |
| fly | flew | flown |
| forget | forgot | forgotten |
| forgive | forgave | forgiven |
| freeze | froze | frozen |
| get | got | got, gotten |
| give | gave | given |
| go | went | gone |
| grind | ground | ground |
| grow | grew | grown |
| hang (a picture) | hung | hung |
| hang (a person) | hanged | hanged |
| hear | heard | heard |
| *heat | heated | heated |
| hide | hid | hidden |
| hit | hit | hit |

| PRESENT TENSE | PAST TENSE | PAST PARTICIPLE |
|---|---|---|
| hold | held | held |
| hurt | hurt | hurt |
| kneel | knelt | knelt |
| know | knew | known |
| lay (to place) | laid | laid |
| lead | led | led |
| leap | leaped, leapt | leaped, leapt |
| leave | left | left |
| lend | lent | lent |
| let | let | let |
| lie (to rest) | lay | lain |
| lie (to tell a lie) | lied | lied |
| light | lighted, lit | lighted, lit |
| lose | lost | lost |
| make | made | made |
| mean | meant | meant |
| meet | met | met |
| mistake | mistook | mistaken |
| pay | paid | paid |
| prove | proved | proved, proven |
| put | put | put |
| *raise | raised | raised |
| read | read | read |
| rid | rid | rid |
| ride | rode | ridden |
| ring | rang | rung |
| rise | rose | risen |
| run | ran | run |
| say | said | said |

| PRESENT TENSE | PAST TENSE | PAST PARTICIPLE |
|---|---|---|
| see | saw | seen |
| seek | sought | sought |
| sell | sold | sold |
| send | sent | sent |
| set | set | set |
| sew | sewed | sewn, sewed |
| shake | shook | shaken |
| shine (glow; gleam) | shone, shined | shone, shined |
| *shine (polish) | shined | shined |
| show | showed | shown, showed |
| shrink | shrank | shrunk |
| sing | sang | sung |
| sink | sank, sunk | sunk |
| sit | sat | sat |
| slay | slew | slain |
| sleep | slept | slept |
| slide | slid | slid |
| sling | slung | slung |
| slink | slunk | slunk |
| sow | sowed | sowed, sown |
| speak | spoke | spoken |
| speed | speeded, sped | speeded, sped |
| spell | spelled, spelt | spelled, spelt |
| spend | spent | spent |
| spit | spit, spat | spit, spat |
| spring | sprang | sprung |
| stand | stood | stood |
| steal | stole | stolen |
| stick | stuck | stuck |

| PRESENT TENSE | PAST TENSE | PAST PARTICIPLE |
|---|---|---|
| sting | stung | stung |
| stink | stank, stunk | stunk |
| strike | struck | struck |
| strive | strove, strived | striven, strived |
| swear | swore | sworn |
| sweat | sweated, sweat | sweated, sweat |
| sweep | swept | swept |
| swim | swam | swum |
| swing | swung | swung |
| take | took | taken |
| teach | taught | taught |
| tear | tore | torn |
| tell | told | told |
| throw | threw | thrown |
| thrust | thrust | thrust |
| understand | understood | understood |
| wake | woke, waked | woken, waked |
| wear | wore | worn |
| weave | wove, weaved | woven, weaved |
| weep | wept | wept |
| win | won | won |
| wind | wound | wound |
| wring | wrung | wrung |
| write | wrote | written |

## Errors to Avoid in Principal Parts of Verbs

Do not confuse the past participle with the past tense.

NO: I *swum* two miles last week.

YES: I *swam* two miles last week.

NO: My shirt *shrunk* in the wash.

YES: My shirt *shrank* in the wash.

Learn the irregular verbs. Do not add regular endings to irregular verb stems.

> NO: She *arised* late on Tuesday
>
> YES: She *arose* late on Tuesday.
>
> NO: The batter *swinged* at the ball.
>
> YES: The batter *swung* at the ball.

Do not confuse the past tense with the past participle. Only the past participle uses helping verbs.

> NO: He must have already *broke* the door.
>
> YES: He must have already *broken* the door.
>
> NO: They had *began* early.
>
> YES: They had *begun* early.

## Problem Solving Example:

Choose the correct form of the verb in parentheses.

a. Our hike was interrupted by a storm, which (strike, struck, strucked, strucken) with great force.

b. The children have already (gone, went) to the park.

c. We have (ate, eaten) at Sal's Restaurant several times.

d. I have (flew, flown) to Los Angeles, California, twice.

e. Susan (forgot, forgotten) she had a paper due in economics today.

f. Scott was (chose, chosen) for the internship at Bell Technologies.

a. *Struck* is the correct answer. The past tense form of *strike* is needed to complete the sentence (*struck*). *Strucked* is incorrect because *-ed* is not added to the past tense of irregular verbs. *Strucken* is incorrect because *-en* is not added to the past tense of *strike*. *Strike* is an irregular verb that has the same form in the past tense and past participle (*struck*)

b. *Gone* is the correct answer. Since the sentence contains the helping verb *have*, the correct verb form is the past participle *gone*.

c. *Eaten* is the correct answer. *Ate* is the past tense of *eat*. *Eaten* is correct because it is the past participle form of *eat*. The past participle is always used with an auxiliary verb.

d. *Flown* is the correct answer. *Flown* is the past participle of *fly*. The past participle is always used with an auxiliary verb, such as *have*. *Flew* is incorrect because *flew* is the past tense of *fly*.

e. *Forgot* is the correct answer. *Forgot* is the past tense of *forget*. *Forgotten* is incorrect because *forgotten* is the past participle of *forget*. The past participle always uses an auxiliary verb.

f. *Chosen* is the correct answer. *Chosen* is the past participle of *choose*. The past participle is always used with an auxiliary verb. *Chose* is incorrect because the sentence contains a helping verb.

## 4.4.2  *Lie* and *Lay* and Other Troublesome Verbs

Do not confuse similar verbs. Two pairs of verbs that often cause trouble are *lie* and *lay* and *sit* and *set*.

| PRESENT | PAST | PAST PARTICIPLE | "ING" FORM |
|---------|------|-----------------|------------|
| Lie (to rest) | lay | lain | lying |
| Lay (to place) | laid | laid | laying |
| Sit (to be seated) | sat | sat | sitting |
| Set (to place) | set | set | setting |

*Lay* and *set* are transitive and always take an object because they refer to something. *Lie* and *sit* are intransitive and stand alone.

NO:   *Lay* down here and rest.

YES:  *Lie* down here and rest.

NO:    The pen is *laying* on the table.

YES:   The pen is *lying* on the table.

NO:    I had *laid* down for a nap

YES:   I had *lain* down for a nap.

NO:    The dog was *setting* there.

YES:   The dog was *sitting* there.

NO:    She *sat* it down on the floor.

YES:   She *set* it down on the floor.

## Problem Solving Example:

Choose the correct form of the verb in parentheses.

a.  When I am tired, I (lay, lie) down for a short nap.

b.  Professor Smith surprised everyone by (sitting, setting) on his desk.

c.  Last night, I (lay, laid) awake on my bed for several hours.

d.  Yesterday, Mrs. Southern (set, sat) the new picture of her granddaughter on her mantle.

e.  When I (lay, laid) my cellular telephone on the circulation desk in the library, someone stole it.

f.  The students who were (sitting, setting) in the front row received backstage passes to meet U2.

a.  *Lie* is the correct answer. *Lie* is the present tense. *Lie* means *to rest. Lay* is incorrect. *Lay* means to place.

b.  *Sitting* is the correct answer. *Sitting* is the -*ing* form of *sit. Sit* means to be seated. *Setting* is incorrect. *Setting* is the -*ing* form of *set. Set* means to place.

c.  *Lay* is the correct answer. *Lay* is the past tense of *lie. Last night* indicates the past tense form of the verb will be needed to complete this sentence. *Laid* is incorrect. *Laid* is the past tense of *lay*, which means *to place.*

d.  *Set* is the correct answer. *Set* means to place. *Yesterday* indicates the past tense will be needed. *Set* does not change forms from the present tense to the past tense. *Sat* is incorrect. *Sat* is the past tense of *sit*. *Sit* means to be seated.

e. *Laid* is correct. *Laid* is the past tense of *lay*. *Lay* means to place. *Lay* is incorrect. *Lay* is the past tense of *lie*. *Lie* means to rest.

f. *Sitting* is the correct answer. *Sitting* is the *-ing* form of the verb *sit*. *Sit* means to be seated. *Setting* is incorrect. *Setting* is the *-ing* form of *set*. *Set* means to place.

## 4.5 Agreement Between Subjects and Verbs

When parts of a sentence agree, there is a logical relationship between them. The most important kind of agreement is between the subject and the verb. The verb must agree with the subject in both number and person. That is, if the subject is singular, the verb must also be; if the subject is plural, the verb must be plural. If the subject is in the third person (*he, she, it, one, they*), the verb must also be in the third person. The main difficulty is identifying the subject of the sentence and determining whether it is singular or plural. (For discussions of how to recognize singular and plural subjects, see *The Noun* and *Pronouns*.)

### 4.5.1 Subjects Followed by Additives

Do not be distracted by words that come between the subject and the verb. Remember to always make the verb agree with the subject of the sentence.

NO: The *arrival* of many friends promise good times.

YES: The *arrival* of many friends promises good times.

NO: *All* the Democrats, including John, *hopes* Murray wins.

YES: *All* the Democrats, including John, *hope* Murray wins.

NO: Every one of you *know* your subject well.

YES: Every one of you *knows* your subject well.

# Problem Solving Example:

Choose the correct form of the verb in parentheses.

a. The couple, happy that the wedding is finally over, (go, goes) to the airport gladly.

b. The seven dogs, even the smallest, (eat, eats) the same amount of food.

c. A color of many hues (is, are) interesting.

d. Stuart, along with Sally, Thomas, and Jordan, (was, were) late to class.

e. The elm, like most trees here, (turn, turns) color in the fall.

f. The sound of the bells always (please, pleases) me.

a. *Goes* is the correct answer. The words *happy that the wedding is finally over* come between the subject *couple* and the verb *goes*. The subject and the verb must agree. The singular subject *couple* agrees with the singular verb form *goes*.

b. *Eat* is the correct answer. The words *even the smallest* come between the subject *dogs* and the verb *eat*. The subject and the verb must agree. The plural subject *dogs* agrees with the plural verb form *eat*.

c. *Is* is the correct answer. The prepositional phrase *of many hues* comes between the subject *color* and the verb *is*. The subject and the verb must agree. The singular subject *color* agrees with the singular verb form *is*.

d. *Was* is correct. The prepositional phrase *along with Sally, Thomas, and Jordan* comes between the subject *Stuart* and the verb *was*. The subject and the verb must agree. The singular subject *Stuart* agrees with the singular verb form *was*.

e. *Turns* is the correct answer. The prepositional phrase *like most trees here* comes between the subject *elm* and the verb *turns.* The subject and the verb must agree. The singular subject *elm* agrees with the singular verb form *turns.*

f.  *Pleases* is the correct answer. The prepositional phrase *of the bells* comes between the subject *sound* and the verb *pleases.* The subject and the verb must agree. The singular subject *sound* agrees with the singular verb form *pleases.*

### 4.5.2 Subjects That Follow Verbs

In sentences in which the subject follows the verb, be especially careful to determine the subject and make it agree with the verb.

NO:  In the back of the room *sits* many of my *friends.*

YES:  In the back of the room *sit* many of my *friends.*

NO:  Into the dark *stares* her black *cats.*

YES:  Into the dark *stare* her black *cats.*

NO:  There *is* many *pictures* on the wall.

YES:  There *are* many *pictures* on the wall.

### 4.5.3 Subjects Joined by Correlative Conjunctions

When singular subjects are joined by *either . . . or, neither . . . nor,* *or,* or *nor,* the verb is singular.

NO:  Either the *principal* or the football *coach* usually *attend* the dance.

YES:  Either the *principal* or the football *coach* usually *attends* the dance.

NO:  I'm sure that neither the *lawyer* nor the *accountant are* to blame.

YES:  I'm sure that neither the *lawyer* nor the *accountant is* to blame.

If one of the subjects is plural and one singular, make the verb agree with the subject nearer it.

NO: Neither the *cat* nor the *dogs is* eating today.

YES: Neither the *cat* nor the *dogs are* eating today.

NO: Either the *students* or the *teacher speak* at any one time in this classroom.

YES: Either the *students* or the *teacher speaks* at any one time in this classroom.

## Problem Solving Example:

Choose the correct form of the verb in parentheses.

a. Either exercise or yoga (is, are) an excellent way to reduce stress.

b. Neither the grass nor the flowers (was, were) growing well.

c. Either her mother or her father (drive, drives) her to school on rainy days.

d. Ann or Rita (has, have) the zoology class notes for today's class.

e. Neither the chorus nor the actors (know, knows) their parts.

a. *Is* is the correct answer. *Either . . . or* is a correlative conjunction. The singular subjects (*exercise*, *yoga*) must have a singular verb form (*is*).

b. *Were* is the correct answer. *Neither . . . nor* is a correlative conjunction. When one subject is singular (*grass*) and the other subject is plural (*flowers*), the verb must agree with the subject nearer it (flowers). A plural subject (*flowers*) must have a plural verb form (*were*).

c. *Drives* is the correct answer. *Either . . . or* is a correlative conjunction. The singular subjects (*mother*, *father*) must agree with the singular verb form (*drives*).

d. *Has* is the correct answer. *Or* is a coordinating conjunction joining singular subjects (*Ann*, *Rita*). A singular subject takes a singular verb form (*has*).

e. *Know* is the correct answer. *Neither . . . nor* is a correlative conjunction. When one subject is singular (*chorus—chorus* is a collective noun and is considered singular in this use) and the other subject is plural (*actors*), the verb agrees with subject nearer it (*actors*). A plural subject takes a plural verb form (*know*).

## 4.5.4  Words Used as Words or Titles

Remember that a word used either as a word or as the title of a particular work, even if it is plural, requires a singular verb.

NO:     *Politics are a noun.*

YES:    *Politics is a noun.*

NO:     The *New York Times print* informative, reliable stories on most subjects.

YES:    The *New York Times prints* informative, reliable stories on most subjects.

## 4.5.5  Other Subjects

The difficulty with collective nouns is trying to decide whether to use the singular or plural verb form. When the emphasis is on the collection, the singular is used, as in

The *orchestra* plays at noon every day.

If the emphasis is on the individual members of the group, the plural verb is required.

The *orchestra* are unable to work well together.

Therefore, the meaning of the sentence determines which form is correct. This problem will be treated in more detail in the discussion of agreement between the subject and the verb.

Collective nouns can be used in the plural form.

The *teams* are ready to begin.

I heard both *orchestras* last night.

Subjects preceded by *each, every, many a,* and *the number of* are singular.

> NO: The *number of* students dropping out of school have increased.
>
> YES: The *number of* students dropping out of school has increased.
>
> NO: *Every* employee have a key to the building.
>
> YES: *Every* employee has a key to the building.

## 4.6 Verbals

**Verbals** are words that originate from verbs. They can be confusing because they are like verbs and, at the same time, like other parts of speech. They have verb forms: the **gerund, infinitive**, and **participle**; and, like verbs, they can show tense, take complements, and be modified by adverbs. They function, however, like other parts of speech: the *noun, adjective,* and *adverb*. In short, verbals are verb forms that do not function as verbs.

### 4.6.1 Gerunds

The **gerund** is a verb form that ends in "ing" and is used as a noun.

> *Writing* a paper is not as easy as you might think.
>
> John's *laughing* in class caused the principal to reprimand him.

The gerund has two tenses: *present* and *perfect.* (The perfect tense refers to action occurring before the action represented by the main verb in the sentence.)

> present: *walking, speaking*
>
> perfect: *having walked, having spoken*
>
> *Eating* all those cookies gave Johnny a stomach ache.
>
> *Having missed* the bus made us late for the concert.

## Problem Solving Example:

**Q** Underline the gerunds in the following sentences.

a. Fighting in school is not allowed.

b. Having graduated from college earned my twin sister and me a vacation to Hawaii.

c. I enjoy walking, for it helps me stay healthy.

d. He is unhappy about having a Monday morning 8 o'clock class.

**A** a. *Fighting* is a gerund.

b. *Having graduated* is a gerund.

c. *Walking* is a gerund.

d. *Having* is a gerund.

### 4.6.2 The Infinitive

The **infinitive** is the base or bare form of the verb, usually preceded by the preposition "to." It may function as a *noun*, an *adjective*, or an *adverb*.

> to write          to run

It is not as easy *to write* a paper as you might think.

*To run* every day requires diligence.

The infinitive also has two tense forms: present and perfect.

> present: *to walk, to speak*
>
> perfect: *to have walked, to have spoken*

Mary had *to walk* to the bus stop.

We were supposed *to have completed* the job by Monday.

## Problem Solving Example:

**Q** Underline the infinitives in the following sentences.

a. Attending a movie is very enjoyable; I usually like to go once a week.

b. Having mowed the grass in the backyard, Chet sat down to drink a glass of water.

c. Completing the novel, the student began to discuss the implications of the plot and its relationship to the theme.

d. I have homework to do, so I can't go to the party.

a. *To go* is an infinitive.

b. *To drink* is an infinitive.

c. *To discuss* is an infinitive.

d. *To do* is an infinitive.

### 4.6.3 The Participle

The **participle** is a verb form that usually ends in "ing" or "ed" or, less frequently, "en," "d," or "t." It functions primarily as an adjective, although it may also serve as an adverb.

The *laughing* boy was silenced by harsh words.

*Frightened*, the little girl hid behind her mother.

The *stolen* purse was retrieved by the police yesterday.

The participle has three tense forms; present, past, and perfect.

Present participle: *walking, speaking*

Past participle: *walked, spoken*

Perfect participle: *having walked, having spoken*

The man *walking* down the street is her uncle.

The paper, *having been written* and *revised*, was ready for publication.

The table, well *constructed*, was on display at the museum.

## Problem Solving Example:

Underline the participles in the following sentences.

a. The woman leaving the building is a well-known business woman.

b. Excited, the college senior walked across the stage to accept his diploma.

c. Dover College, expecting a large number of freshmen, placed three students in each dormitory room.

d. Saddened, the college chaplain announced the deaths of two college students.

a. *Leaving* is a present participle.

b. *Excited* is a past participle.

c. *Expecting* is a present participle.

d. *Saddened* is a past participle.

## 4.7 Voice

**Voice** is the relationship of the subject to the verb, that is, whether the subject is the performer of the action or whether it is the receiver of the action.

### 4.7.1 Active Voice

An **active voice** sentence is one in which the subject is the performer of the action:

The pitcher hit the ball.

Someone stole the jewels.

### 4.7.2 Passive Voice

A **passive voice** sentence is one in which the doer of the action is either unknown or irrelevant; the subject is then the receiver of the action:

The ball was hit by the pitcher.

The jewels were stolen.

In general, use the **active voice** in writing. The **passive voice** should be used only when there are specific stylistic or contextual reasons.

A transitive verb is either active or passive. When the subject acts, the verb is active. Similarly, when the subject is acted upon, the verb is passive.

In writing, the active voice is preferable because it is emphatic and direct. A weak passive verb leaves the doer unknown or seemingly unimportant. However, the passive voice is essential when the action of the verb is more important than the doer, when the doer is unknown, or when the writer wishes to place the emphasis on the receiver of the action rather than on the doer.

*Examples:* Using the active voice rather than the passive.

Weak Passive:  The garbage can was hit by the station wagon.

Strong Active:  The station wagon hit the garbage can.

*Example:* Using the passive voice.

Another man was hired yesterday.

Here, the action of the verb is more important than the doer.

All the buildings were destroyed during the bombing.

In this example, the emphasis is on the receiver of the verb.

## Problem Solving Example:

Indicate whether the following sentences are written in the active or the passive voice by writing active or passive in the blank provided.

a. _____ The man catches poisonous snakes for a living.

b. _____ A light pole was hit by a car.

c. _____ John plans to run for student body president next year.

d. _____ The students protested the small number of summer semester course offerings.

e. _____ The buildings are being renovated by Stewart and Sons Construction Company.

a. This sentence is written in the active voice. The subject of the sentence *man* is performing an action (*catching poisonous snakes*).

b. This sentence is written in the passive voice. The subject of the sentence *pole* is the receiver of the action. (*It was hit by a car.*)

c. This sentence is written in the active voice. The subject of the sentence (*John*) is performing the action (*planning to run for student body president*).

d. This sentence is written in the active voice. The subject of the sentence *students* is performing the action (*protested*).

e. This sentence is written in the passive voice. The subject of the sentence *buildings* is the receiver of the action. (*They are being renovated.*)

## 4.8 Mood

The form or the **mood** of a verb indicates something about the action. In the English language, there are three moods: the indicative, the imperative, and the subjunctive.

**The Indicative Mood:** The indicative mood makes a statement or poses a question.

<blockquote>We are leaving.　　Are we leaving?</blockquote>

**The Imperative Mood:** The imperative mood expresses a command, a request, or a direction.

Don't touch the sculpture.

**The Subjunctive Mood:** The subjunctive mood is used in *that* clauses that express motion, resolution, recommendation, command, or necessity.

I recommend that the plans be carried through.

The subjunctive mood is also used in *if* clauses that express doubt or the impossibility of the condition.

If I had the time, I would join the tennis club.

Lastly, the subjunctive mood is used in main clauses to express hope, wish, or prayer.

God save the queen.

The verb *to be* often gives writers difficulty. In the subjunctive mood, use the verb *to be* as follows:

a.   *Be* in all forms of the present tense.

b.   *Were* in all forms of the past tense.

c.   *Have been* in all forms of the present perfect tense.

## Quiz: The Noun, Pronouns, Expletives, and Verbs

Choose the best word to complete the sentence.

1. Herodotus and Thucydides were both ancient Greek
   _____ , but their styles of recording and analyzing events differed greatly.

   (A) dramatists

   (B) historians

   (C) psychoanalysts

   (D) scientists

2. Susan <u>laid</u> in bed too long and missed her class.

   (A) lays

   (B) lay

   (C) lied

   (D) No change is necessary.

3. The Great Wall of China <u>is</u> fifteen hundred miles long; it <u>was built</u> in the third century B.C.

   (A) was. . .was built

   (B) is. . .is built

   (C) has been. . .was built

   (D) No change is necessary.

4. The ceiling of the Sistine Chapel <u>was</u> painted by Michelangelo; it <u>depicted</u> scenes from the Creation in the Old Testament.

   (A) was. . .depicts

   (B) is. . .depicts

   (C) has been. . .depicting

   (D) No change is necessary.

5. Every man, woman, and child <u>were given</u> a life preserver.

   (A) have been given

   (B) had gave

   (C) was given

   (D) No change is necessary.

6. Hiding your mistakes <u>don't</u> make them go away.

   (A) doesn't

   (B) do not

   (C) have not

   (D) No change is necessary.

7. My friend and <u>myself</u> bought tickets for *Cats*.

   (A) I

   (B) me

   (C) us

(D) No change is necessary.

8. Everyone is wondering <u>whom</u> her successor will be.

(A) who

(B) whose

(C) who'll

(D) No change is necessary.

9. A student <u>who</u> wishes to protest <u>his or her</u> grades must file a formal grievance in the Dean's office.

(A) that. . .their

(B) which. . .his

(C) whom. . .their

(D) No change is necessary.

10. Which of the following sentences contains an expletive?

(A) Please put the blanket over there.

(B) They're not going to be happy about this.

(C) There are many homeless people in this city.

(D) Butterflies sometimes damage their wings.

---

## ANSWER KEY

| | |
|---|---|
| 1. (B) | 6. (A) |
| 2. (B) | 7. (A) |
| 3. (D) | 8. (A) |
| 4. (A) | 9. (D) |
| 5. (C) | 10. (C) |

# CHAPTER 5

# Adjectives and Adverbs

## 5.1 Recognizing Adjectives and Adverbs

Adjectives and adverbs always appear in relation to some other word; they are **modifiers**. They have so much in common that they can be considered together.

*The opposing* team played *an aggressive*, *sophisticated* game.

All of the words italicized above are **adjectives**. You can recognize an adjective because it always modifies a noun, a pronoun, or any other word or group of words playing the part of a noun. Adjectives qualify, describe, or limit nouns or pronouns.

The italicized words in the following sentence are **adverbs**. Adverbs modify verbs, adjectives, or other adverbs.

She thought *deeply* about her *most dearly* loved companion, *then* left *immediately* with a *little* more hope that she could *still* find him *soon*.

As you can see, modifiers are a part of almost all sentences. Although only the subject (noun or pronoun) and the verb are necessary for a complete sentence, such a simple construction is unusual.

"Time flies" is an example of such a minimal expression. Even a short sentence such as "The dog barks" contains a modifier. The more complex a sentence becomes, the more modifiers are used. Modifiers help to make the meaning of a sentence clearer and more exact. A careful study of them is important to good writing.

Sometimes we can recognize a word as an adverb or an adjective by its form, but sometimes the same form of a word is used for both functions. In these cases, it is difficult to distinguish between an adverb and an adjective. One clue is that many adverbs end in "ly." Here is a comparison of the adjectival and adverbial forms of some nouns.

| *NOUN* | *ADJECTIVE* | *ADVERB* |
|--------|-------------|----------|
| truth | truthful | truthfully |
| intention | intentional | intentionally |
| theory | theoretical | theoretically |

Not all adverbs end in *–ly*, and to complicate matters there are a number of adjectives that do.

Examples of adverbs that do not end in *–ly*:

| now | still | quite |
|-----|-------|-------|
| then | when | almost |
| soon | here | very |
| yet | too | often |

*Now* they are ready to be *very* helpful.

Call me *often* if you *still* love me.

Examples of adjectives that end in *–ly*:

| lovely | orderly | timely |
|--------|---------|--------|
| lively | friendly | lonely |

Mary is a *lovely* girl, but her sister Jean is *homely*.

It was a *timely* decision that led to *friendly* relations between the two schools.

Some words have the same form whether they are used as an adjective or an adverb. For example:

| well | deep | right |
|------|------|-------|
| early | fast | wrong |

| little | late | better |
| very | above | hard |
| much | long | |

The difference between adverbs and adjectives actually depends not on distinctive endings but on the way the word functions in a sentence. If the word modifies a noun, it is an adjective. If it modifies an adjective, adverb, or verb, it is an adverb.

Is he *well*? (adjective)

Does he type *well*? (adverb)

*Fast* though he was, he couldn't keep up with Steven. (adjective)

How *fast* can you run? (adverb)

There are some adverbs that have two acceptable forms—one with an –*ly* ending and one without the –*ly* ending. Usually, the –*ly*, or longer form, is preferred—especially for writing. The shortened form is more likely to be used in speaking informally. Examples of these adverbs are

direct—directly      slow—slowly

tight—tightly        close—closely

Though we often drop the –*ly* in speech, this usage is usually not correct and should be avoided.

NO:   Don't talk so *loud*.

YES:  Don't talk so *loudly*.

NO:   You *sure* have all the luck.

YES:  You *surely* have all the luck.

## Problem Solving Example:

Identify the adjectives and/or adverbs in the following sentences.

a.  That was an interesting answer to a difficult question.

b.  He answered the question honestly.

c.  In advanced scuba diving, students swim in deep waters.

 d. Susan almost passed the botany test.

 e. The professor told the student, "That is a likely excuse."

 f. Her grandfather is a jolly old man.

 a. *Interesting* is an adjective that describes the noun *answer*.
  *Difficult* is an adjective that describes the noun *question*.

 b. *Honestly* is an adverb that modifies the verb *answered*.

 c. *Advanced* is an adjective that describes the noun *scuba diving*.
  *Deep* is an adjective that describes the noun *waters*.

 d. *Almost* is an adverb that modifies the verb *passed*. *Botany*
  is an adjective that describes the noun *test*.

 e. *Likely* is an *-ly* adjective that describes the noun *excuse*.

 f. *Jolly* and *old* are adjectives that describe the noun *man*.

## 5.2 Degrees of Adjectives and Adverbs

Adjectives and adverbs have three forms that show a greater or lesser degree of the characteristic of the basic word: the **positive**, the **comparative**, and the **superlative**. The basic word is called the positive. The comparative is used in referring to two persons, things, or groups. The superlative is used to refer to more than two people, things, or groups; it indicates the greatest or least degree of the quality named. Most adjectives of one syllable become comparative by adding "er" to the ending; they become superlative by adding "est" to the ending. In adjectives ending with "y," the "y" changes to "i" before the endings are added.

Examples of comparison of adjectives:

| POSITIVE | COMPARATIVE | SUPERLATIVE |
| --- | --- | --- |
| big | bigger | biggest |
| happy | happier | happiest |
| late | later | latest |
| lovely | lovelier | loveliest |

Adjectives of two or more syllables usually form their comparative degree by adding "more" (or "less"); they form their superlative degree by adding "most" (or "least").

Examples of comparison of adjectives of two or more syllables:

| POSITIVE | COMPARATIVE | SUPERLATIVE |
|----------|-------------|-------------|
| handsome | more handsome | most handsome |
|          | less handsome | least handsome |
| timid    | more timid  | most timid  |
|          | less timid  | least timid |

Some adjectives are irregular; their comparatives and superlatives are formed by changes in the words themselves.

Examples of comparison of irregular adjectives:

| POSITIVE | COMPARATIVE | SUPERLATIVE |
|----------|-------------|-------------|
| good     | better      | best        |
| many     |             |             |
| much     | more        | most        |
| some     |             |             |
| bad      | worse       | worst       |
| little   | less        | least       |
| far      | farther     | farthest    |
|          | further     | furthest    |

Def.:   *Farther* refers to a greater physical distance.
*Further* refers to a greater degree, time, or quality.

Adverbs are compared in the same way as adjectives of more than one syllable: by adding "more" (or "less") for the comparative degree and "most" (or "least") for the superlative.

Examples of comparison of adverbs:

| POSITIVE | COMPARATIVE | SUPERLATIVE |
|----------|-------------|-------------|
| easily | more easily | most easily |
|  | less easily | least easily |
| quickly | more quickly | most quickly |
|  | less quickly | least quickly |

Some adverbs are irregular; some add "er" or "est."

Examples of comparison of irregular adverbs:

| POSITIVE | COMPARATIVE | SUPERLATIVE |
|----------|-------------|-------------|
| little | less | least |
| well | better | best |
| far | farther | farthest |
| badly | worse | worst |
| fast | faster | fastest |
| soon | sooner | soonest |
| much | more | most |

The comparative and superlative indicate not only the differences in the degree of the quality named, but also in the number of things discussed.

Use the comparative to compare two things.

Mary is the *lazier* of the two.

I've tasted *creamier* cheese than this.

Use the superlative to compare more than two things.

Mary is the *laziest* girl I know.

This is the *creamiest* cheese I've ever tasted.

There are some words to which comparison does not apply, because they already indicate the highest degree of a quality. Here are some examples.

Adverbs and adjectives with no comparison:

| | | |
|---|---|---|
| immediately | superlative | first |
| last | very | unique |
| uniquely | universally | perfect |
| perfectly | exact | complete |
| correct | dead | deadly |
| preferable | round | perpendicularly |
| square | third | supreme |
| totally | infinitely | immortal |

### Errors to Avoid in Comparison

Do not combine two superlatives.

> NO:  That was the *most bravest* thing he ever did.

> YES:  That was the *bravest* thing he ever did.

Do not combine two comparatives.

> NO:  Mary was *more friendlier* than Susan.

> YES:  Mary was *friendlier* than Susan.

Do not omit the second *as* in a comparative construction.

> NO:  My lawn is as pretty, if not prettier than, my neighbor's.

> YES:  My lawn is as pretty as, if not prettier than, my neighbor's.

## Problem Solving Example:

Complete the following sentences using the comparative or superlative form of the word in parentheses.

a  John Hilton ran _____ (fast) than his teammate in the relay race.

b.  Throughout high school, Hong and Chen were the _____ (good) in math.

c. That answer is the _____ (less) correct of them all.

d. Valerie read the part _____ (well) than Jane.

e. Craig responded to the interviewer _____ (candidly) than Tom.

f. According to my sorority sisters, Carlos is _____ (handsome) single man in the senior class.

a. *Faster* is the comparative form of the adjective *fast*. The comparative form compares two persons, things, or groups. In this sentence, John is being compared to his teammate. *Fast* is made comparative by adding *er* (faster).

b. *Best* is the superlative form of the adjective *good*. *Good* is an irregular adjective that changes to *best* in the superlative. The superlative form compares more than two persons, things, or groups. In this sentence, Hong and Chen are being compared to all their classmates.

c. *Least* is the superlative form of the adjective *little*. *Little* is an irregular adjective that changes forms in the comparative and superlative. The superlative compares more than two persons, things, or groups. In this sentence, one specific answer is being compared to all the answers.

d. *Better* is the comparative form of the adverb *well*. *Well* is an irregular adverb that changes to *better* in the comparative. The comparative compares two persons, things, or groups. In this sentence, Valerie's reading of the part is being compared to Jane's reading of the part.

e. *Candidly* is an adverb of more than one syllable. To make a word of more than one syllable comparative, the writer must add the word *more* before *candidly*. The comparative compares two persons, things, or groups. In this sentence, Craig responded more candidly than Tom.

f. *Handsome* is an adjective of two syllables and may change its form with either the addition of *-est* or *-most* to the word. The superlative compares more than two persons, things, or groups. In this sentence, Carlos is being compared to all the single men in the senior class.

## 5.3 Comparison with "Other" or "Else" or "Of All"

A common mistake when comparing members of a group is to forget to indicate that the item being held up for comparison is still a part of the rest of the group to which it is being compared. The addition of "other" or "else" to the comparative makes this relationship clearer. If the superlative is used, adding "of all" makes the meaning more definite and emphatic.

> NO: She is a better piano player than any pianist in our group. (*Is she part of the group?*)
>
> YES: She is a better piano player than any other pianist in our group. (*It is now clear that she is a member of the group.*)
>
> NO: Our dog is smarter than any on the block. (*Does the dog live on the block?*)
>
> YES: Our dog is smarter than any other on the block. (*Now it is obvious that the dog lives on the block.*)
>
> NO: Your car is the fastest car in the neighborhood. (*Whose neighborhood?*)
>
> YES: Your car is the fastest of all the cars in the neighborhood (*Your car belongs in the neighborhood.*)

## 5.4 Confusion with Adverbs and Adjectives

### 5.4.1 Linking Verbs

There are two categories of verbs after which an adjectival form is used instead of an adverbial form. When using these verbs, some make the mistake of choosing an adverb instead of an adjective since, logically, the modifier seems to refer to the verb. Actually it refers to the subject.

Use an adjective after:

1.  Forms of the verb "to be" and other nonaction verbs, such as these:

| seem | appear | become |
|------|--------|--------|
| remain | prove | |

The boy was studious. (*studious boy*)

She appears happy. (*happy girl*)

2.  Verbs of the senses, such as these:

| taste | feel | look |
|-------|------|------|
| smell | sound | |

Marianne feels sick. (*sick Marianne*)

That apple tastes good. (*good apple*)

> NO:   Those girls look beautifully. (*wrong*)
> Those girls are beautifully. (*illogical*)

> YES:   She appears happy.
> She is happy. (*logical*)

Sometimes the modifier refers to the verb, describing or clarifying the manner of the action. In this case, the adverbial form must be used.

She *felt cautiously* for the light switch. (*cautiously felt*)

Her parents *appeared immediately* after she called. (*immediately appeared*)

## Problem Solving Example:

Complete the following sentences by using the correct form (adjective or adverb) of the word in parentheses.

a.  I thought to myself, "The solution seems _____ (clear)."

b.  The student looked _____ (diligent) for her lost English literature term paper.

c.  According to the newspaper article, "The driver of the car was hurt _____ (bad)."

d.  After the student congress meeting, my roommate said, "Joe feels _____ (bad)."

e. Campus police arrived _____ (quick) after the fire alarm sounded in the administration building.

a. An adjective (*clear*) is needed after the nonaction verb (*seems*).

b. The adverbial form (*diligently*) is needed after (*looked*), which is used as an intransitive verb in this sentence.

c. An adverb (*badly*) is needed after the action verb (*hurt*).

d. An adjective (*bad*) is needed after a verb of the senses (*feels*).

e. The adverbial form (*quickly*) is needed with the action verb (*arrived*).

## 5.5 Faulty Comparisons

When adjectives and adverbs are used incorrectly in comparisons, the result can be illogical statements.

NO:   The crime rate in Detroit is higher. (higher than what?)

YES:  The crime rate in Detroit is higher than it is in other large cities.

NO:   The crime rate in Detroit is higher than New York. (The crime rate cannot be higher than the city.)

YES:  The crime rate in Detroit is higher than New York's.

## Problem Solving Example:

Determine if the comparison is used correctly in the following sentences. If the comparison is incorrect, write the correction above the line. If the comparison is correct, write Correct in the blank provided.

a. _____ Pizza Chalet's pizza is better than House of Pizza.

b. _____ Gates' Electronics new modem is the fastest modem sold in the United States today.

c. _____ The interest at my loan company is higher than my bank.

d. _____ The crime rate is lower in New York than it is in Chicago.

e. _____ Our football team is as good as any other university's.

a. This sentence is incorrect. Pizza is being compared to a restaurant. Change the sentence to *Pizza Chalet's pizza is better than the pizza at House of Pizza.*

b. This sentence is correct. The sentence says that of all of the modems made in the United States today, a Gates' Electronics modem is the fastest.

c. This sentence is incorrect. The comparison is incorrect because a loan company is being compared to a bank. Change to *The interest at my loan company is higher than my bank's.*

d. This comparison in this sentence is correct.

e. This sentence is correct, the comparison is made clear.

# CHAPTER 6

# Prepositions

## 6.1 Simple Prepositions

*Between* New York and Chicago, we came *upon* two strange signs that kept us *inside* the car *despite* our strong desire to go outside *around* daybreak. *For* hours, we stayed *on* the road *contrary to* our plan, *with* those signs reappearing *before* our eyes long after they had disappeared *from* our sight.

All the italicized words in the preceding paragraph are prepositions. Prepositions are connecting words; they connect the word or words that follow them (called the **object** of the preposition) with some other part of the sentence. They illustrate a relationship between words. The preposition and the word or group of words that follows it constitute the **prepositional phrase**, which can function in a sentence as an adjective, adverb, or noun.

There are two kinds of prepositions—simple, one-word prepositions and group prepositions

| | | |
|---|---|---|
| *at* the office | *by* the seashore | *for* your love |
| *down* south | *on* the desk | *like* her sister |
| *through* the door | *about* the house | *within* three weeks |
| *beside* the bed | *over* the top | *behind* his chair |
| *except* you | *across* town | *with* kind greetings |

## Problem Solving Example:

Underline the prepositions in the following sentences.

a. Spending a quiet evening at home after a long day on the job is wonderful.

b. I found my credit card on the floor behind my dresser.

c. All passengers walked through the security checkpoint at the Midway Airlines gate.

d. Juan lives across town from the amusement park where he works.

e. Valerie placed her English composition notes on the table beside her bed.

a. at, after, on

b. on, behind

c. through, at

d. across, from

e. on, beside

## 6.2 Group Prepositions

| | | |
|---|---|---|
| according to | in conjunction with | in place of |
| because of | as well as | in addition to |
| by means of | in front of | in spite of |
| together with | due to | along with |

There are only a few rules governing the use of prepositions. Learning to use the correct preposition is really a matter of developing a good sense of what sounds right. This is acquired by listening and by trying to write the way we talk. Of course, some aspects of speech must be formalized for writing.

**Errors to Avoid**

In speech, there is a tendency to either overuse or omit necessary prepositions. This usage should be eliminated in formal writing.

Example of overuse:

    NO:    Let's divide *up* the orange.

    YES:   Let's divide the orange.

Example of omission:

    NO:    She was concerned *about* Jamie and his many dogs.

    YES:   She was concerned *about* Jamie and *about* his many dogs.

Need for different prepositions in the same phrase:

    NO:    Mother was both influenced and annoyed *with* her doctor.

    YES:   Mother was both influenced *by* and annoyed *with* her doctor.

Overconcern with placement:

Although in the past it was considered incorrect English to end a sentence with a preposition, it is no longer so. Current usage (everyday speech) and rhythm often necessitate putting a preposition at the end of a sentence. Excessive attention paid to following the outdated rule can result in some unnatural and confusing sentences.

    NO:    Tell me *for* what you are looking.

    YES:   Tell me what you are looking *for*.

## Problem Solving Example:

 Draw a line through any unnecessary preposition or add a preposition where needed in the following sentences.

    a.  She just could not start in to do her political science homework.

    b.  Let's finish up the assignment before tomorrow.

    c.  We should go over to James's house tonight.

    d.  Leland learned of F. Scott Fitzgerald's life and his times through reading his biography.

    e.  Judy always had an interest and an aptitude for science.

a. The preposition *in* is not needed in this sentence.

b. The preposition *up* is not needed in this sentence.

c. The preposition *over* is not needed in this sentence.

d. The preposition *of* should be added before "*his times*" to make the prepositional phrases *of F. Scott Fitzgerald's life* and "of his times" parallel.

e. The preposition *in* should be added after *interest* to make the prepositional phrases *an interest in* and *an aptitude for* parallel.

## 6.3  Idiomatic Use of Prepositions

**Idioms** are expressions that are characteristic of a particular language. The idiomatic use of prepositions has become quite popular in the English language. Here, prepositions are used after certain verbs, participles, nouns, and adjectives. New forms and meanings of these idiomatic prepositions are continually coming into the language. It is advisable to consult the dictionary to determine whether an expression is **idiomatic**, for example, "similar to," or **unidiomatic**, for example, "similar with." Other usage labels, such as informal, vulgar, and slang, should also be checked so that the writer can determine whether the expression is appropriate for that particular piece of writing. The following is a brief list of some standard idiomatic prepositions. For further discussion of idioms, see *Using the Dictionary*.

| | |
|---|---|
| abstain from | empty of |
| acquit of | envious of |
| addicted to | expert in |
| adept at | foreign to |
| adhere to | hint at |
| agree to (a thing) | identical with |
| agree with (a person) | independent of |
| angry at (a thing) | infer from |
| angry with (a person) | inseparable from |
| averse to | jealous of |

| | |
|---|---|
| capable of | oblivious of |
| characteristic of | prerequisite for |
| compare to (for an example) | prior to |
| compare with | proficient in |
| (to illustrate a point) | profit by |
| concern in | prohibit from |
| concerned with | protest against |
| desire for | reason with |
| desirous of | regret for |
| devoid of | repugnant to |
| differ about | sensitive to |
| differ from (things) | separate from |
| differ with (a person) | substitute for |
| different from | superior to |
| disagree with | sympathize with |
| disdain for | tamper with |
| distaste for | unmindful of |

## 6.4    List of Common Prepositions

| | | |
|---|---|---|
| about | before* | down |
| above | behind | during |
| across | below | except |
| after* | beneath | for |
| against | beside | from |
| along (with) | between | in |
| amid | beyond | including |
| among | but | inside |
| around | by | into |
| as* | concerning | like |
| at | despite | near |

| | | |
|---|---|---|
| off | through | up |
| on | throughout | up to |
| out | till | upon |
| outside | to | versus |
| over | toward | via |
| past | towards | with |
| regarding | under | within |
| round | underneath | without |
| since* | until* | worth |

*also used as subordinating conjunctions

# CHAPTER 7

# Conjunctions

## 7.1 Coordinating Conjunctions

*Not only* Susan *but also* both Andrew *and* Samuel were *either* for fighting *or* for getting out immediately, *since* no help had arrived. *Although* they all wanted to stay, the fighting was bound to begin again, *and* this time with more force *than* before.

The italicized words in the preceding paragraph are all conjunctions. Like prepositions, **conjunctions** are connecting words. They connect words, phrases, or clauses. There are four kinds of conjunctions: coordinating conjunctions, conjunctive adverbs, correlative conjunctions, and subordinating conjunctions.

Coordinating conjunctions connect sentences and parts of a sentence that are equivalent. It is fairly simple to determine whether sentence parts are equivalent: words are equal to other words; phrases are equal to phrases; main clauses are equal to main clauses; and minor (or subordinating) clauses are equal to minor clauses. The following are commonly used coordinating conjunctions:

| and | but | yet | so |
|-----|-----|-----|-----|
| for | or | nor | |

They may join a word to another word.

| Mom *and* Dad | Jill *or* Susan | firm *yet* kind |
|---|---|---|

A phrase to another phrase:

of great insight *but* of poor judgment

A minor (subordinate) clause to another minor clause:

She insisted that she knew him *yet* (that she) had not told him the story.

A main clause to another main clause:

I wanted to attend the meeting, *but* John never had the slightest intention of going.

The old grammar rule that said never start a sentence with *and* or *but* is no longer adhered to. Sometimes using a coordinating conjunction to start a sentence is very effective.

She said she would leave early. *And* she did.

## Problem Solving Example:

Identify the coordinating conjunctions in the following sentences.

   a. Linda and her sister attended the Bon Jovi concert.

   b. I wanted to read the book, but I could not find it in the library.

   c. They decided to go to the beach or go to the movies.

   d. We were on time. But she was late.

   e. I wanted to be a nurse, so I enrolled in the nursing program at Montgomery College.

   a. *And* is a coordinating conjunction. *And* joins one word (*Linda*) to another word (*her sister*).

   b. *But* is a coordinating conjunction. *But* joins one main clause (*I wanted to read the book*) to another main clause (*I could not find it in the library*).

   c. *Or* is a coordinating conjunction. *Or* joins the phrase (*to the beach*) to another phrase (*to the movies*).

d. *But* is a coordinating conjunction. *But* begins the second main clause (*She was late*).

e. *So* is a coordinating conjunction. *So* joins one main clause (*I wanted to be a nurse*) to another main clause (*I enrolled in the nursing program at Montgomery College*).

### 7.1.1 Parallel Structures with Conjunctions

When using a coordinating conjunction, be sure that the sentence elements you are joining are equivalent.

No: Her main interests were *that she succeed and skiing.*

Yes: Her main interests were *success* and *skiing.*

OR

Yes: Her main interests were that she *succeed* and *that she ski regularly.*

## 7.2 Conjunctive Adverbs

**Conjunctive adverbs** have a dual role. They connect independent clauses and also illustrate the relationship between the two clauses. Although the clause introduced by the conjunctive adverb is grammatically sufficient, a logical relationship exists with the other clause. Since the conjunctive adverb basically introduces a modifying clause, it is less of a connector than the coordinating conjunctions.

Clauses joined by conjunctive adverbs must be separated by either a period or a semicolon. The following are some conjunctive adverbs and transitional phrases, which serve the same function.

| | | |
|---|---|---|
| therefore | furthermore | nevertheless |
| however | besides | indeed |
| consequently | moreover | thus |
| accordingly | still | hence |
| for this reason | likewise | on the contrary |

| | | |
|---|---|---|
| for example | in addition | in the first place |
| on the other hand | at the same time | then |

He won the competition in Moscow; *consequently*, he went on to have an outstanding career as a soloist.

He had shown a great deal of potential; *and for this reason*, he was given the job.

His essay provided many fine insights. *Moreover*, it was well written.

## Problem Solving Example:

Identify the conjunctive adverbs in the following sentences.

a. John trained thoroughly for the event; moreover, he won first place.

b. I had to run to catch the bus; nevertheless, I was late for work.

c. I do not dislike John. On the contrary, he is one of my best friends.

d. Judith read the novel; however, she did not enjoy it.

e. I want to buy a car. Therefore, I must save money for the down payment.

a. *Moreover* is a conjunctive adverb. *Moreover* connects two independent clauses. The first independent clause is *John trained thoroughly for the event*. The second independent clause is *He won first place*.

b. *Nevertheless* is a conjunctive adverb. *Nevertheless* joins two independent clauses. The first independent clause is *I had to run to catch the bus*. The second independent clause is *I was late for work*.

c. *On the contrary* is a conjunctive adverb. *On the contrary* begins the independent clause *he is one of my best friends*.

d. *However* is a conjunctive adverb. *However* joins two

independent clauses. The first clause is *Judith read the novel.* The second independent clause is *She did not enjoy it.*

e. *Therefore* is a conjunctive adverb. *Therefore* begins the second independent clause *I must save money for the down payment.*

## 7.3 Correlative Conjunctions (used in pairs)

These conjunctions are always used in pairs that illustrate clearly that the parts they connect in a sentence are equivalent (parallel). The correlative conjunctions are

| | |
|---|---|
| both . . . and | not only . . . but also |
| either . . . or | neither . . . nor |
| if . . . then | whether . . . or |

The parts they join must be similar in form.

Either *the secretary or the treasurer* must preside.

**Errors to Avoid**
When correlative conjunctions are used, a commonly made mistake is forgetting that each member of the pair must be followed by the same kind of construction.

NO:  Her reaction not only *was strong* but also *immediate.*

YES:  Her reaction not only was *strong* but also was *immediate.*

OR

YES:  Her reaction was not only *strong* but also *immediate.*

## Problem Solving Example:

Identify the correlative conjunctions in the following sentences.

a. Mary not only won the race but also set a record.

b. If you apologize, then I will help you with your geography project.

c. Either you make a decision or you forget the offer.

d. Following the press conference, neither the congressman nor his aide could be reached for comment.

e. Both the mayor and the city council are against the property tax increase.

a. *Not only . . . but also* are the correlative conjunctions. The correlative conjunctions join *won* to *set.*

b. *If . . . then* are the correlative conjunctions. The correlative conjunctions join the two clauses.

c. *Either . . . or* are the correlative conjunctions. The correlative conjunctions join *you make a decision* to *you forget the offer.*

d. *Neither . . . nor* are the correlative conjunctions. The correlative conjunctions join *congressman* to *aide.*

e. *Both . . . and* are the correlative conjunctions. The correlative conjunctions join *mayor* to *city council.*

## 7.4   Subordinating Conjunctions

Not all sentences are composed solely of equal parts. Usually there are some parts that are essential to the main idea and some others that serve as support or give additional information about the main idea. Subordinating conjunctions are used to help connect parts of a sentence that are unequal. Some subordinating conjunctions are

| | | | |
|---|---|---|---|
| as | because | as though | even though |
| since | although | through | till |
| provided that | after | before | whenever |
| in order that | when | while | wherever |
| until | if | unless | whereas |
| how | so that | that | as soon as |
| where | as if | as long as | |

Typically, these words introduce descriptive (subordinate) clauses and connect them to the main clauses. For example:

I'll go with you *provided that* you drive.

*Because* she ran quickly, she arrived on time.

Faulty coordination can also be corrected by placing ideas of lesser importance in a subordinate position.

NO: He did not practice driving, *and* he failed his road test.

YES: *Because* he did not practice driving, he failed his road test.

NO: The election returns came in Tuesday night *and* weren't published in the morning paper.

YES: *Although* the election returns came in Tuesday night, they weren't published in the morning paper.

## Problem Solving Example:

 Identify the subordinating conjunction in the following sentences.

a. Until you came, there was no one to help with the dishes.

b. He smiled as though he had won the contest.

c. I finished the calculus problems before John had a chance to get started.

d. He was not satisfied although he checked his test answers twice.

e. Since I was a child, I have always wanted to live in New York City.

 a. *Until* is the subordinating conjunction. *Until* introduces the subordinate clause *Until you came* and connects the subordinate clause to the main clause *there was no one to help with the dishes.*

b. *As though* is the subordinating conjunction. *As though* introduces the subordinate clause *as though he had won the contest* and connects the subordinate clause to the main clause *he smiled.*

c. *Before* is the subordinating conjunction. *Before* introduces the subordinate clause *before John had a chance to get started* and connects it to the main clause *I finished the calculus problems.*

    d. *Although* is the subordinating conjunction. *Although* introduces the subordinate clause *although he checked his test answers twice* to the main clause *He was not satisfied.*

    e. *Since* is the subordinating conjunction. *Since* introduces the subordinate clause *Since I was a child* and connects the subordinate clause to the main clause *I have always wanted to live in New York City.*

## 7.4.1 Relative Pronouns Used as Subordinating Conjunctions

Relative pronouns may also be used to introduce subordinate clauses: *who, whom, which, where, that.*

**Other Errors to Avoid**

Improper use of *while*:

*While* refers to time and should not be used as a substitute for *although, and,* or *but.*

    NO:    *While* I'm usually interested in Fellini movies, I'd rather not go tonight.

    YES:   *Although* I'm usually interested in Fellini movies, I'd rather not go tonight.

## Quiz: Adjectives & Adverbs, Prepositions, and Conjunctions

**DIRECTIONS:** Choose the correct option.

    1. Although the band performed <u>badly</u>, I feel <u>real bad</u> about missing the concert.

    (A) badly. . .real badly

    (B) bad. . .badly

    (C) badly. . .very bad

    (D) No change is necessary.

2. He did <u>very well</u> on the test although his writing skills are not <u>good</u>.

    (A) real well. . .good

    (B) very good. . .good

    (C) good. . .great

    (D) No change is necessary.

**DIRECTIONS:** Select the sentence that clearly and effectively states the idea and has no structural errors.

3. (A) Los Angeles is larger than any city in California.

    (B) Los Angeles is larger than all the cities in California.

    (C) Los Angeles is larger than any other city in California.

    (D) Los Angeles is larger than the cities in California.

4. (A) Art history is as interesting as, if not more interesting than, music appreciation.

    (B) Art history is as interesting, if not more interesting than, music appreciation.

    (C) Art history is as interesting as, if not more interesting, than music appreciation.

    (D) Art history is as interesting as, if not more interesting as, music appreciation.

5. (A) The baseball team here is as good as any other university.

(B) The baseball team here is as good as all the other universities.

(C) The baseball team here is as good as any other university's.

(D) The baseball team here is as good as the other universities.

6. (A) I like him better than you.

(B) I like him better than I like you.

(C) I like him better.

(D) I like him more than you.

7. (A) You are the most stingiest person I know.

(B) You are the most stingier person I know.

(C) You are the stingiest person I know.

(D) You are the more stingiest person I know.

8. Which of the underlined words in the following sentence is the conjunction?

Although I knew it was going to rain, I foolishly left all of the windows open in my house.

(A) although

(B) going

(C) foolishly

(D) open

9. Joe stated that the class began at 10:30 a.m.

(A) on

(B) from

(C) to

(D) No change is necessary.

10. The statue looks very different _____ the way it used to look.

    (A) then

    (B) than

    (C) from

    (D) to

## ANSWER KEY

| | |
|---|---|
| 1. (C) | 6. (B) |
| 2. (D) | 7. (C) |
| 3. (C) | 8. (A) |
| 4. (A) | 9. (D) |
| 5. (C) | 10. (C) |

# Parts of the Sentence

## 8.1 Subject and Predicate

A **sentence** is a group of words that makes sense, ending with a period, exclamation point, or question mark. It is the basic unit of communication. Every sentence, unless it is a command, has a subject and a predicate.

| SUBJECT | PREDICATE |
|---------|-----------|
| Harry | drives his father's truck. |
| We | saw a flock of geese. |
| Elephants | never forget. |

The **subject** is the topic of the sentence. It announces what the sentence is about. The **predicate** is what is said about the subject. The subject is generally a noun or pronoun, as in the examples above. Sometimes gerunds, infinitives, phrases, and clauses can also act as the subject. When they do, they are called **nominals** (a word or group of words that acts like a noun).

*His singing* woke the whole house.

*What we don't* know is his age.

*To fly* has always been man's dream.

Commands have no apparent subject. Because of the nature of the command, it is tacitly understood to be *you*.

Run as fast as you can!

Add up these numbers and tell me the answer.

Jeff, please buy me a newspaper. (Jeff is the person addressed, not the subject.)

*Compound subjects* are two or more simple subjects connected by *and* or *or*.

*Music and dancing* followed dinner.

*Check or money order* must accompany each application.

The *complete subject* is the simple subject and all its modifiers.

*The women who sang at the party* left on the 5:00 train.

*A few Cadillacs* were parked outside the building.

The predicate always contains a verb. The *simple predicate* is the verb without any modifiers.

Gail *laughed*.

The gorillas *bellowed*.

Edgar Allan Poe *wrote* some rather grim stories.

A *compound predicate* is two simple predicates connected by *and* or *or*.

The audience *shouted and clapped* when the curtain fell.

You either *saw* the film or *heard* about it.

## Problem Solving Example:

Identify the subjects and predicates in the following sentences.

a.  Susan cultivated the garden.

b.  The man in the brown suit is an undercover policeman.

c.  Time and practice helped her win the long jump competition.

d.  I laughed and cried when I won the lottery.

e.  My two friends standing over there are graduating next year.

f.  Fix the leak immediately.

a. *Susan* is the subject. *Cultivated* is the predicate.

b. *Man* is the subject. *Is* is the predicate. *In the brown suit* is a prepositional phrase that comes between the subject and the predicate and modifies the subject.

c. *Time and practice* is the subject. *Time and practice* is a compound subject made up of two simple subjects (*time, practice*) joined by *and*. The predicate is *helped*.

d. *I* is the subject of the main clause. *Laughed and cried* is the predicate. *Laughed and cried* is a compound predicate made up of two simple predicates (*laughed, cried*) joined by *and*. *I* is the subject of the subordinate clause; *won* is the predicate.

e. *Friends* is the subject. *Are graduating* is the predicate. *Standing over there* is a participial phrase that comes between the subject and the predicate and modifies *friends*.

f. *You* is the understood subject of this imperative sentence. *Fix* is the predicate.

## 8.2   Sentence Order

Usually the parts of the sentence appear in this order:

*SUBJECT—VERB—DIRECT OBJECT*

| James | smokes | cigars |
| Bill | collects | lizards. |

If there is an indirect object, it appears in front of the direct object:

*SUBJECT—VERB—INDIRECT OBJECT—DIRECT OBJECT*

| Harry | saved | me | some chicken |

If the verb is intransitive or copulative (linking), the order is:

*SUBJECT—VERB—COMPLEMENT*

| Marie | laughs | excessively. |
| George | is | a good businessman. |

Of course, sentences do not always have words in this order.

Commands, for example, have no subject.

*VERB—OBJECT*

Drive    the car.

Milk    the cow.

The order of parts may be altered in a question. The example below gives the question in SUBJECT—VERB—DIRECT OBJECT order, then shows a few alternatives.

Plato wrote *The Republic?*

(*VERB—SUBJECT—OBJECT*)

Did Plato write *The Republic?*

(*VERB—SUBJECT—OBJECT*)

Was *The Republic* written by Plato?

(*VERB—SUBJECT—COMPLEMENT*)

The use of expletives will also change word order. *It* and *there*, when used as introductory words, are *expletives*. They fill the space of the subject, but an expletive is never the actual subject of a sentence.

There are bears in the woods nearby.

(*VERB—SUBJECT—COMPLEMENT*)

It is good for brothers to live in peace.

(*VERB—COMPLEMENT—SUBJECT*)

Word order is also changed for emphasis:

We cleaned the house quickly. (*normal order*)

The house we cleaned quickly. (*emphasis on "the object house"*)

Birds and airplanes were in the sky. (*normal order*)

In the sky were birds and airplanes. (*emphasis on the phrase "in the sky"*)

We crept to the window quietly, like thieves. (normal order)

Quietly, like thieves, to the window we crept. (*emphasis on how we were creeping*)

These changes in word order, especially the last example—for emphasis—add variety and color to writing.

## Problem Solving Example:

 Identify the parts of the following sentences by writing subject, predicate, direct object, indirect object, and complement.

a. He drives the car cautiously.

b. John called me to apologize.

c. The dog barks loudly.

d. Read the book.

e. They gave the money to Joe.

a. *He* is the subject. *Drives* is the predicate. *The car* is direct object. *Cautiously* is the adverbial modifier.

b. *John* is the subject. *Called* is the predicate. *Me* is the direct object. *To apologize* is the infinitive phrase used as an adverb.

c. *The dog* is the subject. *Barks* is the predicate. *Loudly* is the adverbial complement.

d. *Read* is the complement. *The book* is the direct object. *You* is understood to be the subject of the command.

e. *They* is the subject. *Gave* is the predicate. *The money* is the direct object. *To Joe* is the prepositional phrase used as an adverb.

# CHAPTER 9

# Phrases

## 9.1 Prepositional Phrases

"So young a child," said the gentleman *sitting opposite to her* (he was dressed *in white paper*), "ought to know which way she's going, even if she doesn't know her own name!"

A Goat that was sitting *next to the gentleman in white* shut his eyes and said *in a loud* voice, "She ought to know her way *to the ticket-office*, even if she doesn't know her alphabet!"

—Lewis Carroll, *Through the Looking Glass*

All the italicized groups of words are phrases. Phrases fill in many of the details that make a sentence interesting. For example, the sentence "*We sat.*" could turn into any of the following by the addition of phrases:

We sat for hours, looking at the painting.

On the cliffs by the sea we sat, watching the sunset.

We sat by Amelia at the restaurant.

A **phrase** is a group of connected words without a subject or predicate. A **prepositional phrase** begins with a preposition and contains a noun and its modifiers. Some examples are as follows:

Take me *to the opera*.

The noun in a prepositional phrase is called the *object of the preposition*.

A prepositional phrase can be used as an adjective:

The woman *on the phone* is Jane.

an adverb:

A large rabbit dove *under the ground.*

or a noun:

*In the evening* is as good a time as any.

## Problem Solving Example:

 In the following sentences, underline the prepositional phrase(s). Then, label each preposition and each object of the preposition.

    a. The woman on the billboard is Bonnie Blair, a famous athlete.

    b. The Career Development Office helped me with my job search.

    c. On the campus map, the computer science building is behind the math building.

    d. I left my sweater in the biology lab.

    e. The chocolate cake in the refrigerator should be saved for tomorrow.

 a. *On the billboard* is a prepositional phrase. *On* is the preposition. *Billboard* is the object of the preposition.

    b. *With my job search* is the prepositional phrase. *With* is the preposition. *Job search* is the object of the preposition.

    c. *On the campus map* is the prepositional phrase. *On* is the preposition. *Campus map* is the object of the preposition. *Behind the math building* is the prepositional phrase. *Behind* is the preposition. *Math building* is the object of the preposition.

    d. *In the biology lab* is the prepositional phrase. *In* is the preposition. *Lab* is the object of the preposition.

e. *In the refrigerator* is the prepositional phrase. *In* is the preposition. *Refrigerator* is the object of the preposition. *For tomorrow* is the prepositional phrase. *For* is the preposition. *Tomorrow* is the object of the preposition.

## 9.2  Gerund Phrases

A **gerund phrase** contains a gerund and its modifiers. It is always used as a noun.

*Reading blueprints* is not as easy as it sounds. (gerund phrase as subject)

Thoreau placed great value on *living simply.* (gerund phrase as object of the preposition *on*)

*Exercising regularly* is *seizing an opportunity to keep healthy.* (gerund phrase as subject and as predicate nominative)

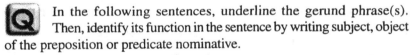

## Problem Solving Example:

 In the following sentences, underline the gerund phrase(s). Then, identify its function in the sentence by writing subject, object of the preposition or predicate nominative.

　　a. Thinking about the future is important to all college seniors.

　　b. College students believe in living cheaply on campus.

　　c. Using computers is a popular way to teach college composition today.

　　d. Susan plans to complete her college education by taking two classes and by interning at a Fortune 500 company.

　　e. Reading newspapers is helping students understand current events.

　　a. *Thinking about the future* is a gerund phrase used as a subject.

　　b. *Living cheaply* is a gerund phrase used as object of the preposition *in*.

c. *Using computers* is a gerund phrase used as a subject.

d. *Taking two classes* is a gerund phrase used as object of the preposition *by. Interning at a Fortune 500 company* is a gerund phrase used as object of the preposition *by.*

e. *Reading newspapers* is a gerund phrase used as a subject.

## 9.3 Infinitive Phrases

An **infinitive phrase** contains an infinitive and its modifiers. It can also be used as a noun, an adjective, or an adverb.

A waiter's job is *to serve a table.* (noun)

Tom brought a book *to lend me.* (adjective)

We'll have to run *to catch the train.* (adverb)

No one had time *to complete the extra-credit problem.* (infinitive phrase used as an adjective modifying the noun *time*)

We left early *to arrive on time.* (infinitive phrase as an adverb, modifying the verb *left*)

We hope *to win the race.* (infinitive phrase as object of verb)

The *present infinitive* also expresses the future time.

We hope *now* to win the race *in the future.*

## Problem Solving Example:

**Q** Underline the infinitive phrase in the following sentences.

Then, identify its function by writing noun, adjective, or adverb in the blank provided.

a. _____ The police want to solve the crime and to maintain justice.

b. _____ Tom bought a rose to give his girlfriend.

c. _____ A librarian's job is to help patrons with their information needs.

d. _____ The best place to study is in a quiet room.

e. _____ The writing tutor's job is to help students improve their writing skills.

a. *To solve the crime* and *to maintain justice* are the infinitive phrases. They are used as direct objects of the verb *want*.

b. *To give his girlfriend* is the infinitive phrase. It is used as an adjective to modify the noun *rose*.

c. *To help patrons with their information needs* is an infinitive phrase used as the predicate nominative/subject complement of the sentence.

d. *To study* is an infinitive used as an adjective modifying *place*.

e. *To help students improve their writing skills* is an infinitive phrase used as a predicate nominative.

## 9.4 Participial Phrases

A **participial phrase** contains a participle and its modifiers. It is used as an adjective to modify a noun or a pronoun.

*Having missed the bus*, we arrived at the party late. (participial phrase as modifier)

The gentleman *standing in the aisle* is the owner.

*The gentleman . . .* (The participial phrase modifies *gentleman*. The prepositional phrase modifies *standing*.)

*Walking the balance beam*, she was extremely careful. (The participial phrase modifies *she*. *Balance beam* is the direct object of the participle *walking*.)

*Running into the house*, Mary tripped on the rug. (*Running into the house* is the participial phrase. But the prepositional phrase *into the house* is also a part. It modifies the participle *running*. The participial phrase modifies *Mary*. *House* is the object of the preposition *into*.)

Incorrect use of a participial phrase results in a stylistic error called a **dangling participle**. For further information on such phrases, see the section *Dangling Modifiers*.

## Problem Solving Example:

Underline the participial phrases in the following sentences.
a. Reading the book, Susie fell asleep.
b. The student, checking his e-mail, noticed a message from his business professor.
c. Having parked the car, we went into the theater.
d. The basketball player running down the court used to play for the Italian National Team.
e. Having left my sweater at the restaurant, I returned to get it the next day.

a. *Reading the book* is the participial phrase. It modifies the subject *Susie*.
b. *Checking his e-mail* is the participial phrase. It modifies the subject *student*.
c. *Having parked the car* is the participial phrase. It modifies the subject *we*.
d. *Running down the court* is the participial phrase. It modifies the subject *player*.
e. *Having forgotten my sweater at the restaurant* is the participial phrase. It modifies the subject *I*.

## 9.5   Absolute Phrases

An **absolute phrase** is one that is related to a sentence in meaning, though it has no grammatical relationship to the sentence. Its form is usually a noun followed by either a prepositional phrase or a participial phrase and other optional modifiers.

The reunion was planned for summer, *summer being the time of year when most people take vacations.*

*The play having ended,* everyone left the theater.

CHAPTER **10**

## Clauses

## 10.1 Independent and Subordinate Clauses

A **clause** differs from a phrase in that it has a subject and a predicate.

PHRASE: We're planning a trip *to the museum*.

CLAUSE: We're planning a trip *so that we can see the museum*.

PHRASE: *After a swim*, we'll have lunch.

CLAUSE: *After we swim*, we'll have lunch.

**Independent/main clauses** are those which can stand alone as sentences.

We lost the game. We smiled like winners.

We lost the game, but we smiled like winners.

**Dependent/subordinate clauses** are those which cannot stand alone as sentences. They are introduced by either a subordinating conjunction or a relative pronoun used as a subordinating conjunction. Subordinate clauses may function as adverbs, adjectives, or nouns.

An **adverb clause** functions as an adverb and usually begins with subordinating conjunctions like *as, as if, as though, than, if, until, since, before, because, after, while, when*, and *so that*.

*Although we lost the game*, we smiled like winners.

An **adjective clause** functions as an adjective and usually begins with a relative pronoun like *who, whom, whose, which, where,* or *that* (often omitted).

The game *we lost* was the semifinal in the state championship. ("that" is omitted)

The game, *which was held in the gymnasium,* generated a lot of excitement in the community.

A **noun clause** functions as a noun; it may serve as the subject of a sentence, the subject complement, or the object. Interrogative pronouns like *how, what, who, whom,* and *whose* usually introduce noun clauses.

*What you don't know* won't hurt you. (The noun clause is the subject of the sentence.)

What you see is *what you get.* (The second noun clause is the subject complement of the sentence.)

You already know *who I am.* (The noun clause is the direct object of the transitive verb "know.")

## Problem Solving Example:

Indicate if the italicized portion is a dependent clause or an independent clause in the blank provided.

a. _____ They left the house early *so that they could get a good seat in the theater.*

b. _____ *If I won the lottery,* I would take a cruise.

c. _____ *While students were taking their abnormal psychology test,* the instructor left the classroom.

d. _____ Cindy will attend Towson State, and *she will major in accounting.*

e. _____ The world literature class was dismissed early *because the instructor became ill during class.*

f. _____ The weatherman forecasted sunny warm weather, *yet temperatures were cool.*

a. *So that* is a subordinating conjunction that joins the dependent clause *so that they could get a good seat in the theater* to the independent clause *they left the house early.*

b. *If* is a subordinating conjunction that begins the dependent clause *if I won the lottery.* A dependent clause cannot stand alone as a sentence.

c. *While* is a subordinating conjunction that begins a dependent clause *While the students were taking their abnormal psychology test.* A dependent clause cannot stand alone as a sentence.

d. *And* is a coordinating conjunction that connects the independent clauses. An independent clause can stand alone as a sentence.

e. *Because* is a subordinating conjunction which introduces the subordinate clause *because the instructor became ill during class.*

f. *Yet* is a coordinating conjunction that connects the independent clauses. An independent clause can stand alone as a sentence.

## 10.2 Elliptical Clauses

An **elliptical clause** is one in which words that are necessary for grammatical completeness but not for meaning are not used.

My sister is older *than I [am].*

*While [I was] walking home,* I met my sister.

*When [you are] in Rome,* do as the Romans do.

## Problem Solving Example:

Underline the elliptical clauses in the following sentences.

a. Though hungry, the dog was quiet.

b. My brother plays piano better than I.

c. While walking to class, I lost my calculator.

d. When leaving your dormitory at night, you should tell someone where you are going.

      a. *Though hungry*

      b. *Than I*

      c. *While walking to class*

      d. *When leaving your dormitory at night*

---

## Quiz: Parts of the Sentence, Phrases, and Clauses

**DIRECTIONS:** In the following, which part of the sentence is the underlined word?

1. <u>Susan</u> cultivated the garden.

   (A) Subject

   (B) Infinitive Phrase

   (C) Predicate

   (D) Independent Clause

2. <u>Reading the book,</u> she fell asleep.

   (A) Participial Phrase

   (B) Infinitive Phrase

   (C) Gerund

   (D) Prepositional Phrase

3. Only a few people <u>knew</u> the answer to that question.

   (A) Gerund

   (B) Subject

   (C) Predicate

   (D) Participle

4. <u>Scott</u> wrote a letter to Mary.

   (A) Predicate

   (B) Subject

   (C) Object

   (D) Gerund

5. The police set out <u>to solve the crime</u> and to maintain justice.

   (A) Subject

   (B) Direct Object

   (C) Predicate

   (D) Infinitive Phrase

6. The woman <u>on the billboard</u> over there is a famous athlete.

   (A) Infinitive Phrase

   (B) Direct Object

   (C) Predicate

   (D) Prepositional Phrase

7. <u>She</u> drives the car slowly.

   (A) Subject

   (B) Prepositional Phrase

   (C) Indirect Object

   (D) Predicate

8. <u>John moved the dresser next to the door</u> before painting the bedroom.

   (A) Direct Object

   (B) Predicate

   (C) Dependent Clause

   (D) Independent Clause

9. My car, <u>which is parked outside</u>, is blue.

   (A) Independent Clause

   (B) Dependent Clause

   (C) Predicate

   (D) Subject

10. The man, <u>having painted the house</u>, took a rest.

    (A) Predicate

    (B) Participial Phrase

    (C) Gerund

    (D) Prepositional Phrase

## ANSWER KEY

| | |
|---|---|
| 1. (A) | 6. (D) |
| 2. (A) | 7. (A) |
| 3. (C) | 8. (D) |
| 4. (B) | 9. (B) |
| 5. (D) | 10. (B) |

# CHAPTER 11

## Sentence Errors—
## Structural Problems

### 11.1 Dangling Modifiers

The **dangling modifier** (which includes participles, infinitives, and gerunds) leaves the verbal without or in search of a subject to modify. The sentence lacks clarity, and the reader must take a moment to determine the writer's intention. The most common kind of dangling modifier is the dangling participle.

    NO:    At age six, my father taught me to swim.

    YES:  When I was six, my father taught me to swim.

    NO:    After showing the experiment, it was time to go home.

    YES:  After he showed us the experiment, we had to go home.

    NO:    The door was shut while dancing with Debbie.

    YES:  The door was shut while I was dancing with Debbie.

The difficulty with the sentences above is that the reader is not sure who is doing what. *"The door was shut while dancing with Debbie"* is ambiguous. *Who* is dancing with Debbie? The door? It is important to be clear about the sense of every sentence. Meaning can be completely changed when a word or phrase is moved into or out of the proper place.

Modifiers (participles, infinitives, and gerunds—verbals) usually dangle because, as in some of the examples above, the verbal is in search of a subject to modify.

## 11.2 Misplaced Modifiers

There are other types of modifiers that cause confusion when they are out of place. It is not important to learn the names of the various errors one could make, but it is important to avoid such errors. In general, structure a sentence logically by placing the modifier near the word it modifies. In each of the following examples, a phrase is out of place.

> NO: I saw two stores and a movie theater walking down the street.
>
> YES: Walking down the street, I saw two stores and a movie theater.
>
> NO: Harold watched the painter gaping in astonishment.
>
> YES: Harold watched the painter and gaped in astonishment. Gaping in astonishment, Harold watched the painter.
>
> NO: You can see the moon standing in the front yard.
>
> YES: If you stand in the front yard, you can see the moon. Standing in the front yard, you can see the moon.

There are some words that must always be placed immediately before the word they modify, or they will cause confusion. These are words like *almost, only, just, even, hardly, nearly, not,* and *merely.*

> NO: Jane almost polished the plate until it shined.
>
> YES: Jane polished the plate until it almost shined.
>
> NO: The store on the corner only sells that toaster.
>
> YES: Only the store on the corner sells that toaster.

Look at how the meaning can change when the modifier is moved around in the following series of sentences.

> Only life exists on earth. (*There is nothing else on earth except life.*)

Life only exists on earth. (*Life does nothing but exist on earth.*)

Life exists only on earth. (*Nowhere else but on earth can one find life.*)

Life exists on earth only. (*More emphatic than the last sentence but says the same thing*)

Place *only* and other modifiers close to the word that they modify. This is the best way to avoid ambiguity.

## 11.2.1 Split Infinitives

A **split infinitive** occurs when a modifier is placed between the sign of the infinitive "to" and the verb (*to better serve you*). In the italicized example, the infinitive "to serve" is split by the adverb "better." Careful writers try to avoid splitting infinitives. For example:

Try to *not* split an infinitive.

The patient hopes to *fully* recover from pneumonia.

We want to *better* serve you.

## 11.2.2 Squinting Modifiers

A **squinting modifier** is one which is ambiguous because it is not clear whether it refers to the noun preceding it or the one following it.

NO:  Women who like him sometimes gave him gifts.

YES:  Women who like him gave him gifts sometimes.

NO:  The professor sees juniors only on Fridays.

YES:  The professor sees only juniors on Fridays.

## Problem Solving Example:

Identify the italicized modifier as being a dangling modifier or a misplaced modifier by writing dangling modifier or misplaced modifier in the blank provided. If the sentence is correct, write Correct in the blank provided.

a. _____ He discovered a new route *driving home.*

b. _____ *After sitting at the computer all day,* my back was sore.

c. _____ He ran a mile *although his ankle was sprained.*

d. _____ *Running to the bus,* Esmerelda's heel on one of her shoes broke.

e. _____ We saw two girls riding bicycles *from our car.*

f. _____ *While Richard was studying in the library,* he lost his research notes for his history paper.

a. *Driving home* is a misplaced modifier. It should be placed before the word it modifies *He.* The corrected sentence should read, *Driving home, he discovered a new route.*

b. *After sitting at the computer all day* is a dangling modifier. It seems to be modifying *my back* instead of the person. The corrected sentence should read, *After sitting at the computer all day, I had a sore back.*

c. This sentence is correct.

d. *Running to the bus* is a dangling modifier. It seems to be modifying *heel.* The corrected sentence should read, *While Esmerelda was running to the bus, the heel on one of her shoes broke.*

e. *From our car* is a misplaced modifier. The modifier should be placed near the subject *we.* The corrected sentence should read, *From our car, we saw two girls riding bicycles.*

f. The sentence is correct. The modifier *While Richard was studying in the library* refers to the subject *he.*

## 11.3 Lack of Parallel Structure

When ideas are similar, they should be expressed in similar forms. When elements of a sentence are similar, they too should appear in similar form.

NO:   She likes sun, the sand, and the sea.

YES:  She likes the sun, the sand, and the sea.

NO:   George is always singing, drumming, or he will play the guitar.

YES:  George is always singing, drumming, or playing the guitar.

NO:   Charlene's car skidded, turned sideways, then comes to a stop.

YES:  Charlene's car skidded, turned sideways, and came to a stop.

Whenever *and* or *or* is used in a sentence, each must connect equal parts. Words are paired with words, phrases with phrases, clauses with clauses, and sentences with sentences. All these pairs must be *parallel*; they must have the same form.

NO:   Her family went to London, to Amsterdam and they even saw Rome and Paris.

YES:  Her family went to London, to Amsterdam, and even to Rome and Paris.

NO:   You can use this form to apply or if you want to change your status.

YES:  You can use this form to apply or to change your status.

NO:   Debby noticed the way Margie talked and how she kept looking at the desk.

YES:  Debby noticed how Margie talked and how she kept looking at the desk.

Pairs of connectives, such as *both . . . and, either . . . or, neither . . . nor,* and *not only . . . but also,* usually connect parallel structures.

NO:   That book was both helpful and contained a lot of information.

YES:  That book was both helpful and informative.

NO:   So, my father said, "Either you come with us now, or stay here alone."

YES: So, my father said, "Either you come with us now, or you stay here alone."

NO: Here we either turn left or right, but I forget which.

YES: Here we turn either left or right, but I forget which.

NO: Karen bought the table both for beauty and utility.

YES: Karen bought the table for both beauty and utility.

## Problem Solving Example:

Proofread the following sentences for errors in parallel structure. Then, correct the error above the line.

a. In the summer, I like swimming and to water ski.

b. Mary read the book, studied the example, and she took the test.

c. The movie was interesting and had a lot of excitement.

d. As a child, Harold told his mother that he wanted to be a fireman, a policeman, and a person who fixes cars.

e. The college's ice cream shop serves three flavors of ice cream: strawberries, vanilla, and chocolate.

a. The words *swimming* and *to water ski* are not parallel. *To water ski* should be changed to *water skiing* to make the phrase parallel with *swimming*.

b. Two verb phrases, *read the book* and *studied the example* are connected to the same clause. Change *she took the test* to *took the test*.

c. *Had a lot of excitement* is not parallel with *interesting. Had a lot of excitement* should be changed to *exciting* to make the words parallel.

d. *A person who fixes cars* is not parallel with *a fireman* or *a policeman. A person who fixes cars* should be changed to *a mechanic* to make it parallel with *a fireman* and *a policeman*.

e. *Strawberries* is not parallel with *vanilla* and *chocolate*. *Strawberries* should be changed to *strawberry* to make it parallel with *vanilla and chocolate*.

## 11.4 Sentence Fragments

"Where did you go?"

"To the new movie theater. The one on Valley Street."

"Where on Valley Street?"

"Just past the train station, and across the street from the post office."

"See a good movie?"

"The best. Really funny, but serious, too."

"Sounds good."

Probably neither of the people in the conversation above realized that they were not using complete sentences. Only the first question, *"Where did you go?"* is a complete sentence. The rest are **sentence fragments**.

A sentence fragment is only a part of a sentence, because it is usually missing a subject or a verb.

NO:   So illogical!

YES:   It is so illogical!

NO:   Only for love, you see.

YES:   They did it only for love, you see.

NO:   No one. Not even the teacher.

YES:   No one, not even the teacher, could do it.

In conversation (as in the one above), there is a tendency to speak in sentence fragments, and so such fragments often appear in our writing. Proofreading and revision, however, can help to correct this error.

There are two ways to correct a sentence fragment. The first is to supply whatever is missing, as was done above. The other way is to attach the fragment to the sentence before or after it.

NO: When I jog, especially in the early morning. I sometimes see the morning star.

YES: When I jog, especially in the early morning, I sometimes see the morning star.

NO: Because he was wrong. That's why he was embarrassed.

YES: He was embarrassed because he was wrong.

NO: Always and everywhere. She thought of him.

YES: Always and everywhere, she thought of him.

It is not always incorrect to use sentence fragments. They are used to reproduce conversation and are also quite effective as questions and exclamations. Some examples are

How absurd!

Now for some examples.

After all this? Not on your life!

The more we studied, the less we knew.

Although properly used sentence fragments can add spark, it is generally best to avoid using them except when more liveliness is needed.

## Problem Solving Example:

Determine if the following word groups are sentence fragments or complete sentences by writing fragment or sentence in the blank provided.

a. _____ After the rain stopped.

b. _____ Sally broke her mother's favorite vase.

c. _____ In the middle of campus behind the administration building.

d. _____ Tom having attended City College for two years.

e. _____ I decided to specialize in pediatrics when I entered medical school.

a. *After the rain stopped* is a fragment. The word group is a dependent clause.

b. This word group is a complete sentence. *Sally* is the subject. *Broke* is the verb.

c. *In the middle of campus behind the administration building* is a fragment composed of two prepositional phrases (*in the middle of campus* and *behind the administration building*).

d. *Tom having attended City College for two years* is a fragment. It is an absolute phrase and lacks a predicating/finite verb.

e. This word group is a complete sentence. *I* is the subject. *Decided* is the verb.

## 11.5 Run-On Sentences

A **run-on sentence** contains two complete sentences totally fused.

NO: It was a pleasant drive the sun was shining.

YES: It was a pleasant drive because the sun was shining.

NO: They are all similar materials they may not look or feel alike.

YES: They are all similar materials, although they may not look or feel alike.

NO: Susan said we passed the restaurant I think it's farther ahead.

YES: Susan said we passed the restaurant. I think it's farther ahead.

## 11.6 Comma Splices

The run-on sentence is a very common error. Sometimes a writer will try to correct it by inserting a comma between the clauses, but this creates another error, a **comma splice**. The following examples illustrate various ways to correct the comma splice.

NO:   Talk softly, someone is listening.

YES:  Talk softly; someone is listening.

OR

Talk softly because someone is listening.

NO:   If you know, you must tell us, we will do it.

YES:  If you know, you must tell us. Then we will do it.

NO:   Take a hint from me, drive more slowly on this curve.

YES:  Take a hint from me: drive more slowly on this curve.

NO:   We were lost, the captain could not see the land.

YES:  We were lost. The captain could not see the land.

## Problem Solving Example:

**Q** Identify the following word groups as being a run-on, comma splice, or sentence by writing run-on, comma splice, or sentence in the blank provided.

a. _____ The settlement was reached on Thursday it seems fair.

b. _____ It was impossible to telephone my mother in St. Petersburg, Florida, the lines were down because of the hurricane.

c. _____ The crowd cheered, for the girls' softball team had won the state finals.

d. _____ Everyone saw the crime, no one was willing to come forth with information.

e. _____ The new semester starts in September I will be taking six classes.

f. _____ Because I enjoy working with preschool children, I decided to major in early childhood education.

a. This word group is a run-on. The first independent clause is *The settlement was reached on Thursday*. The second independent clause is *it seems fair*.

b. This word group is a comma splice. The comma incorrectly separates two independent clauses. The first independent clause is *It was impossible to telephone my mother in St. Petersburg, Florida.* The second independent clause is *the lines were down because of the hurricane.*

c. This sentence is correct. Two independent clauses are joined by a comma, and a coordinating conjunction. The first independent clause is *The crowd cheered.* The second independent clause is *the girls' softball team had won the state finals.*

d. This word group is a comma splice. The comma incorrectly separates two independent clauses. The first independent clause is *Everyone saw the crime.* The second independent clause is *no one was willing to come forth with information.*

e. This word group is a run-on. The first independent clause is *The new semester starts in September.* The second independent clause is *I will be taking six classes.*

f. This word group is a complete sentence. *Because* is a subordinating conjunction that introduces the subordinate clause *Because I enjoy working with children.* The introductory subordinate clause is set off with a comma.

## 11.7  Short, Choppy Sentences—Sentence Variation

Try to read the following passage:

*There was a table set out under a tree. It was in front of the house. The March Hare and the Hatter were having tea at it. A Dormouse was sitting between them. He was fast asleep. The other two were using it as a cushion. They rested their elbows on it. They talked over its head. "Very uncomfortable for the Dormouse," thought Alice; "only, as it's asleep, I suppose it doesn't mind."*

Notice how quickly you read when the sentences are short; you hardly have enough time to form a picture of the scene. It is as if the writer added each thought as it occurred to him, and in fact, this is usually the case. It is a sure sign of poor writing. Now read the same excerpt the way that Lewis Carroll wrote it.

*There was a table set out under a tree in front of the house, and the March Hare and the Hatter were having tea at it: a Dormouse was sitting between them, fast asleep, and the other two were using it as a cushion, resting their elbows on it and talking over its head. "Very uncomfortable for the Dormouse," thought Alice; "only, as it's asleep, I suppose it doesn't mind."*

Sentence variation creates well-balanced, smooth writing that flows and gives the reader the feeling that the writer knows the subject. Although there is nothing grammatically wrong with short sentences, they often separate ideas that should be brought together.

NO:     People change. Places change. Alan felt this. He had been away for ten years.

YES:    On returning after a ten-year absence, Alan had a strong feeling of how people and places change.

NO:     She looked at the sky. Then she looked at the sea. They were too big. She threw a rock in the ocean. She started to cry. Then she went home.

YES:    The sky and the sea looked too big. She threw a rock into the ocean, and as it disappeared she began to cry. Then she turned to go home.

As a rule, avoid using chains of short, choppy sentences. Organize your thoughts and try to vary the length of your sentences.

## 11.8 Wordiness

Effective writing means concise writing. **Wordiness**, on the other hand, decreases clarity of expression by cluttering sentences with unnecessary words. Of course, short sentences are not necessarily better than long ones simply because they are brief. As long as a word serves a function, it should remain in the sentence. However, repetition of words, sounds, and phrases should be used only for emphasis or other stylistic reasons. Editing your writing will reduce its bulk. Notice the difference in impact between the first and second sentences in the following pairs.

NO:    The medical exam that he gave me was entirely complete.

YES:    The medical exam he gave me was complete.

NO:    It seems perfectly clear to me that although he went and got permission from the professor, he still should not have played that awful, terrible joke on the dean.

YES:    It seems clear to me that although he got permission from the professor, he still should not have played that terrible joke on the dean.

NO:    It will be our aim to ensure proper health care for each and every one of the people in the United States.

YES:    Our aim will be to ensure proper health care for all Americans.

## 11.9 Rambling Sentences

A **rambling sentence** continues on and on and seems to never end.

NO:    The mountain was steep, but the road was clear; the sun was shining, and we all had the spirit of adventure in our heart and a song of the open road on our lips, so we took the turn that took our car up that steep mountain road.

YES:    The mountain was steep, but the road was clear. The sun was shining. All of us had the spirit of adventure in our heart and a song of the open road on our lips. So we took our car up that steep mountain road.

There is often nothing grammatically wrong with a rambling sentence; it is simply too long, and it interferes with the reader's comprehension. Unfortunately, a writer who makes this kind of error tends to do it a lot.

CHAPTER 12

## Glossary of Usage

## 12.1 Words Commonly Confused and Misused

The complex nature of language sometimes makes writing difficult. Words often become confusing when they have similar forms and sounds. Indeed, an author may have a correct meaning in mind, but an incorrect word choice can alter the meaning of a sentence or even make it totally illogical.

NO: Martha was always part of that *cliché*.

YES: Martha was always part of that *clique*. (*A cliché* is a trite or hackneyed expression; a *clique* is an exclusive group of people.)

NO: The minister spoke of the soul's *immorality*.

YES: The minister spoke of the soul's *immortality*. (*Immorality* means wickedness; *immortality* means imperishable or unending life.)

NO: Where is the nearest *stationary* store?

YES: Where is the nearest *stationery* store? (*Stationary* means immovable; *stationery* is paper used for writing.)

On the following page are groups of words that are often confused because of their similar forms and sounds.

1. **a**       *A* is used before words beginning with a consonant sound.

   **an**      *An* is used before words with a vowel sound. This distinction is important; it is not the spelling that determines whether to use *a* or *an*, but the sound.

   | | |
   |---|---|
   | an umbrella | BUT a university |
   | a radio | BUT an RCA record |
   | an hour | BUT a human being |
   | a historical event | BUT an honorary degree |

2. **accent**      v. to stress or emphasize. (You must *accent* the last syllable.)

   **ascent**      n. a climb or rise. (John's *ascent* of the mountain was dangerous.)

   **assent**      n. consent, compliance. (We need your *assent* before we can go ahead with the plans.)

3. **accept**      v. to take something offered. (She *accepted* the gift.)

   **except**      prep. other than, but. (Everyone was included in the plans *except* him.)

4. **advice**      n. opinion given as to what to do or how to handle a situation. (Her sister gave her *advice* on what to say at the interview.)

   **advise**      v. to counsel. (John's guidance counselor *advised* him on which colleges to apply to.)

5. **affect**      v. to influence. (Mary's suggestion did not *affect* me.)

   **effect**      v. to cause to happen. (The plan was *effected* with great success.) n. result. (The *effect* of the medicine is excellent.)

6. **allusion**      n. indirect reference. (In the poem, there are many biblical *allusions*.)

   **illusion**      n. false idea or conception; belief or opinion not in accord with the facts. (Greg was under the *illusion* that he would win the race after missing three weeks of practice.)

| | | |
|---|---|---|
| 7. | already | adv. previously. (I had *already* read that novel.) |
| | all ready | adv. + adj. prepared. (The family was *all ready* to leave on vacation.) |
| 8. | altar | n. table or stand used in religious rites. (The priest stood at the *altar*.) |
| | alter | v. to change. (Their plans were *altered* during the strike.) |
| 9. | as if | conj. as it would be if. (It looks *as if* it's going to rain.) |
| | like | prep. inclined to. (It looks *like* rain.) |
| 10. | capital | n. 1. a city where the government meets. (The senators had a meeting in Albany, the *capital* of New York.) 2. money used in business. (They had enough *capital* to develop the industry.) |
| | capitol | n. building in which the legislature meets. (Senator Brown gave a speech at the *capitol* in Washington.) |
| 11. | choose | v. to select. (Which camera did you *choose*?) |
| | chose | past tense, choose. (Susan *chose* to stay home.) |
| 12. | cite | v. to quote. (The student *cited* evidence from the text.) |
| | site | n. location. (They chose the *site* where the house would be built.) |
| 13. | clothes | n. garments. (Because she got caught in the rain, her *clothes* were wet.) |
| | cloths | n. pieces of material. (The *cloths* were used to wash the windows.) |
| 14. | coarse | adj. rough, unrefined. (Sandpaper is *coarse*.) |
| | course | n. 1. path of action. (She did not know what *course* would solve the problem.) 2. passage. (We took the long *course* to the lake.) 3. series |

of studies. (We both enrolled in the physics *course*.) 4. part of a meal. (She served a five-*course* meal.)

| | | |
|---|---|---|
| 15. | consul | n. a person appointed by the government to live in a foreign city and represent the citizenry and business interests of the native country there. (The *consul* was appointed to Naples, Italy.) |
| | council | n. a group used for discussion or advisement. (The *council* decided to accept his letter of resignation.) |
| | counsel | v. to advise. (Tom *counsels* Jerry on tax matters.) |
| 16. | criterion | n. (singular) standard. (The only *criterion* is patience.) |
| | criteria | (plural). (There are several *criteria* applicants must meet.) |
| 17. | decent | adj. proper; respectable. (He was very *decent* about the entire matter.) |
| | descent | n. 1. moving down. (In Dante's *Inferno*, the *descent* into hell was depicted graphically.) 2. ancestry. (He is of Irish *descent*.) |
| 18. | device | n. 1. plan; scheme. (The *device* helped her win the race.) 2. invention. (We bought a *device* that opens the garage door automatically.) |
| | devise | v. to contrive. (He *devised* a plan so John could not win.) |
| 19. | emigrate | v. to go away from a country. (Many Japanese *emigrated* from Japan in the late 1800s.) |
| | immigrate | v. to come into a country. (Her relatives *immigrated* to the United States after World War I.) |
| 20. | eminent | n. prominent. (He is an *eminent* member of the community.) |
| | imminent | adj. impending. (The decision is *imminent*.) |

|  | immanent | adj. existing within. (Maggie believed that a religious spirit is *immanent* in human beings.) |
| 21. | fair | adj. 1. beautiful. (She was a *fair* maiden.) 2. just. (She tried to be *fair*.) n. festival. (There were many games at the *fair*.) |
|  | fare | n. amount of money paid for transportation. (The city proposed that the subway *fare* be raised.) |
| 22. | farther | adv. distance. (We traveled *farther* than we expected.) |
|  | further | adv. furthermore; in depth. (We will discuss this *further*.) |
| 23. | forth | adv. onward. (The soldiers moved *forth* in the blinding snow.) |
|  | fourth | adj. 4th. (She was the *fourth* runner-up in the beauty contest.) |
| 24. | imply | v. to suggest something. (I *implied* that I didn't approve of their actions.) |
|  | infer | v. to draw a conclusion from a remark or action. (I *inferred* from your letter that you will not be attending the meeting next week.) |
| 25. | insure | v. to guarantee. (He *insured* his luggage before the flight.) |
|  | ensure | v. to make certain. (*Ensure* your safety by driving carefully.) |
| 26. | its | possessive form of *it*. (Our town must improve *its* roads) |
|  | it's | contraction of *it is*. (*It's* time to leave the party.) |
| 27. | later | adj., adv. at a subsequent date. (We will take a vacation *later* this year.) |
|  | latter | n. second of the two. (Susan can visit Monday or Tuesday. The *latter*, however, is preferable.) |
| 28. | lead | n. a metal. (The handgun was made of *lead*.) v. to show the way. (The camp counselor leads |

the way to the picnic grounds.)

| | | |
|---|---|---|
| | led | past tense of verb *lead*. (The dog *led* the way) |
| 29. | lend | v. to let out for temporary use. (We are in the business of *lending* you money.) |
| | loan | n. money lent at interest. (The bank gave the student a *loan* for her tuition.) |
| 30. | loose | adj. free, unrestricted. (The dog was let *loose* by accident.) |
| | lose | v. to suffer the loss of. (He was afraid he would *lose* the race.) |
| 31. | moral | adj. virtuous. (She is a *moral* woman with high ethical standards.) n. lesson taught by a story, incident, etc. (Most fables end with a *moral*.) |
| | morale | n. mental condition. (After the team lost the game, their *morale* was low.) |
| 32. | of | prep. from. (She is *of* French descent.) |
| | off | adv. away, at a distance. (The television fell *off* the table.) |
| 33. | passed | past tense of verb *pass*, having satisfied some requirement. (He *passed* the test.) |
| | past | adj. gone by or elapsed in time. (His *past* deeds got him in trouble.) n. a period of time gone by. (His *past* was shady.) prep. beyond. (She ran *past* the house.) |
| 34. | personal | adj. private. (Jack was unwilling to discuss his childhood; it was too *personal*.) |
| | personnel | n. staff. (The *personnel* at the department store was made up of young adults.) |
| 35. | principal | n. head of a school. (The *principal* addressed the graduating class.) adj. main most important. (JR was the *principal* character in the TV drama "Dallas.") or (The country's *principal* export is coffee.) |
| | principle | n. the ultimate source, origin, or cause of |

something; a law, truth. (The *principles* of physics were reviewed in class today.)

36. prophecy — n. prediction of the future. (His *prophecy* that he would become a doctor came true.)

    prophesy — v. to declare or predict. (He *prophesied* that we would win the lottery.)

37. quiet — adj. still; calm. (At night, all is *quiet*.)

    quite — adv. really, truly. (She is *quite* a good singer.)

    quit — v. to free oneself. (Peter had little time to spare, so he *quit* the chorus.)

38. respectfully — adv. with respect, honor, esteem. (He declined the offer *respectfully*.)

    respectively — adv. in the order mentioned. (Jack, Susan, and Jim, who are members of the club, were elected president, vice president, and secretary, *respectively*.)

39. stationary — adj. immovable. (The park bench is *stationary*.)

    stationery — n. paper used for writing. (The invitations were printed on yellow *stationery*.)

40. straight — adj. not curved. (The road was *straight*.)

    strait — adj. restricted, narrow, confined. (The patient was put into a *strait* jacket.) n. narrow waterway. (He sailed through the *Straits* of Magellan.)

41. than — conj. used most commonly in comparisons. (Maggie is older *than* I.)

    then — adv. soon afterward. (We lived in Boston; *then* we moved to New York.)

42. their — possessive form of *they*. (That is *their* house on Tenafly Drive.)

    they're — contraction of *they are*. (*They're* leaving for California next week.)

| | | |
|---|---|---|
| | there | adv. at that place. (Who is standing *there* under the tree?) |
| | | expletive. (There are good teachers at my school.) |
| 43. | to | prep. in the direction of; toward. (She made a turn *to* the right onto Norman Street.) |
| | too | adv. 1. more than enough. (She served *too* much for dinner.). 2. also. (He is going to Maine *too*.) |
| | two | n. 2; the sum of one plus one. (We have *two* pet rabbits.) |
| 44. | weather | n. the general condition of the atmosphere. (The *weather* is expected to be clear on Sunday.) |
| | whether | conj. if it be a case or fact. (We don't know *whether* the trains are late.) |
| 45. | who's | contraction of *who is* or *who has*. (*Who's* willing to volunteer for the night shift?) |
| | whose | possessive form of *who*. (*Whose* book is this?) |
| 46. | your | possessive form of *you*. (Is this *your* seat?) |
| | you're | contraction of *you are*. (I know *you're* going to do well on the test.) |

## Quiz: Sentence Errors—Structural Problems and Glossary of Usage

**DIRECTIONS:** Choose the correct option.

1. His <u>principal</u> reasons for resigning were his <u>principles</u> of right and wrong.

   (A) principal. . .principals

(B) principle. . .principals

(C) principle. . .principles

(D) No change is necessary.

2. All students are <u>suppose to</u> pass the test before <u>achieving</u> upper-division status.

(A) suppose to. . .achieving

(B) suppose to. . .being achieved

(C) supposed to. . .achieving

(D) No change is necessary.

**DIRECTIONS:** Select the sentence that clearly and effectively states the idea and has no structural errors.

3. (A) The student depended on his parents for financial support.

(B) The student lacked the ways and means to pay for his room and board, so he depended on his parents for this kind of money and support.

(C) The student lacked the ways and means or the where-withal to support himself, so his parents provided him with the financial support he needed.

(D) The student lacked the means to pay for his room and board, so he depended on his parents for financial support.

**DIRECTIONS:** Choose the sentence that expresses the thought most clearly and that has no error in structure.

4. (A) Many gases are invisible, odorless, and they have no taste.

(B) Many gases are invisible, odorless, and have no taste.

(C) Many gases are invisible, odorless, and tasteless.

(D) Many gases are invisible and odorless and have no taste.

5. (A) The mayor will be remembered because he kept his campaign promises and because of his refusal to accept political favors.

   (B) The mayor will be remembered because he kept his campaign promises and because he refused to accept political favors.

   (C) The mayor will be remembered because of his refusal to accept political favors and because he kept his campaign promises.

   (D) The mayor will be remembered because of his refusal to accept political favors and that he kept his campaign promises.

6. (A) While taking a shower, the doorbell rang.

   (B) While I was taking a shower, the doorbell rang.

   (C) While taking a shower, someone rang the doorbell.

   (D) The doorbell rang, while taking a shower.

**DIRECTIONS:** Choose the correct option.

7. Nothing grows as well in Mississippi as <u>cotton. Cotton</u> being the state's principal crop.

   (A) cotton, cotton

   (B) cotton; cotton

   (C) cotton cotton

   (D) No change is necessary.

8. It was a heartwrenching <u>movie: one</u> that I had never seen before.

   (A) movie and

   (B) movie, one

(C) movie. One

(D) No change is necessary.

9. Traffic was stalled for three miles on the <u>bridge. Because</u> repairs were being made.

(A) bridge because

(B) bridge; because.

(C) bridge, because

(D) No change is necessary

10. The ability to write complete sentences comes with <u>practice writing</u> run-on sentences seems to occur naturally.

(A) practice, writing

(B) practice. Writing

(C) practice and

(D) No change is necessary.

## ANSWER KEY

| | |
|---|---|
| 1. (D) | 6. (B) |
| 2. (C) | 7. (A) |
| 3. (A) | 8. (B) |
| 4. (C) | 9. (A) |
| 5. (B) | 10. (B) |

# CHAPTER 13

## End Punctuation Marks

### 13.1 The Period

Try to read this paragraph.

*Take some more tea the March Hare said to Alice very earnestly Ive had nothing yet Alice replied in an offended tone so I cant take more you mean you cant take less said the Hatter its very easy to take more than nothing Lewis Carroll*

Now try again.

*"Take some more tea," the March Hare said to Alice, very earnestly.*

*"I've had nothing yet," Alice replied in an offended tone, "so I can't take more."*

*"You mean you can't take less," said the Hatter. "It's very easy to take more than nothing."*

—Lewis Carroll

This example illustrates to what extent punctuation helps the reader understand what the writer is trying to say. The most important role of punctuation is clarification.

In speech, words are accompanied by gesture, voice, tone, and rhythm that help convey a desired meaning. In writing, it is punctuation alone that must do the same job.

There are many rules about how to use the various punctuation marks. These are sometimes difficult to understand because they are described with so much grammatical terminology. Therefore, this discussion of punctuation will avoid as much terminology as possible. If you still find the rules confusing, and your method of punctuation is somewhat random, try to remember that most punctuation indicates the place where pauses should occur in speech.

Keeping this in mind, read your sentences aloud as you write; if you punctuate according to the pauses in your voice, you will do much better than if you put in your commas, periods, and dashes either at random or where they look good.

The three ways to end a sentence are with:

1.   a period
2.   a question mark
3.   an exclamation point

**Periods** end all sentences that are not questions or exclamations. In speech, the end of a sentence is indicated with a full pause. The period is the written counterpart of this pause.

Go get me my paper. I'm anxious to see the news.

Into each life some rain must fall. Last night some fell into mine.

When a question is intended as a suggestion and the listener is not expected to answer, or when a question is asked indirectly as part of a sentence, a period is also used.

Mimi wondered if the parade would ever end.

Will you please send the flowers you advertised.

We'll never know who the culprit was.

Periods also follow most abbreviations and contractions.

| Wed. | Dr.   | Jr.  | Sr.  |
| ---- | ----- | ---- | ---- |
| etc. | Jan.  | Mr.  | Ms.  |
| Esq. | cont. | a.m. | A.D. |

Periods (or parentheses) are also used after a letter or number in a series.

            a. apples                 1. president
            b. oranges                2. vice president
            c. pears                  3. secretary

**Errors to Avoid**

Be sure to omit the period after a quotation mark preceded by a period. Only one stop is necessary to end a sentence.

She said, "hold my hand." (no period after the final quotation mark)

"Don't go into the park until later."

"It's not my fault," he said. "She would have taken the car anyway."

After many abbreviations, particularly those of organizations or agencies, no period is used (check in a dictionary if in doubt).

| AFL-CIO | NAACP | GM |
| FBI | NATO | IBM |
| TV | UN | HEW |

## 13.2 The Question Mark

Use a **question mark** to end a direct question even if it is not in the form of a question. The question mark in writing denotes the rising tone of voice used to indicate a question in speech. If you read the following two sentences aloud, you will see the difference in tone between a statement and a question composed of the same words.

Mary is here.

Mary is here?

Here are some more examples of correct use of the question mark. Pay special attention to the way it is used with other punctuation.

Where will we go next?

"Won't you," he asked, "please lend me a hand?"

"Will they ever give us our freedom?" the prisoner asked.

Who asked, "When?"

Question marks indicate a full stop and lend a different emphasis to a sentence than do commas. Compare these pairs of sentences.

Was the sonata by Beethoven? or Brahms? or Chopin?

Was the sonata by Beethoven or Brahms or Chopin?

Did they walk to the park? climb the small hill? take the bus to town? or go skating out back?

Did they walk to town, climb the small hill, take the bus to town, or go skating out back?

Sometimes question marks are placed in parentheses. This indicates doubt or uncertainty about the facts being reported.

The bombing started at 3 a.m. (?)

She said the dress cost $200,000. (?)

Harriet Stacher (18(?)-1914) was well thought of in her time.

## 13.3 The Exclamation Point

An **exclamation point** ends an emphatic statement. It should be used only to express strong emotions, such as surprise, disbelief, or admiration. If it is used too often for mild expressions of emotion, it loses its effectiveness.

Let go of me!

Help! Fire!

It was a wonderful day!

What a beautiful woman she is!

Who shouted "Fire!" (*Notice no question mark is necessary*)

Fantastic!

"Unbelievable!" she gasped. (*Notice no comma is necessary*)

"You'll never win!" he cried.

Where else can I go! (*The use of the exclamation point shows that this is a strong statement even though it is worded like a question.*)

Do not overuse exclamation points. The following is an example of the overuse of exclamation points:

*Dear Susan,*

*I was so glad to see you last week! You looked better than ever! Our talk meant so much to me! I can hardly wait until we get together again! Could you believe how long it has been! Let's never let that happen again! Please write as soon as you get the chance! I can hardly wait to hear from you!*

*Your friend,*

*Nora*

### 13.3.1 Interjections

An **interjection** is a word or group of words used as an exclamation to express emotion. It need not be followed by an exclamation point. Often an interjection is followed by a comma (see *The Comma*) if it is not very intense. Technically, the interjection has no grammatical relation to other words in the sentence; yet it is still considered a part of speech.

*Oh dear*, I forgot my keys again.

*Ah*! Now do you understand?

*Ouch*! I didn't realize that the stove was hot.

*Oh*, excuse me. I didn't realize that you were next on line.

## Problem Solving Example:

Add periods, question marks, or exclamation points wherever needed.

    a. When will the lecture on college students and eating disorders begin

    b. In September, Mr Morgan will be transferred to the company's plant in Springfield, Ohio

c. Seeing flames coming from the building, the woman shouted, "Call 911"

    d. The college freshman asked. "Where is the library"

    e. As Dr. Smith walked toward her office, she noticed her office door was ajar She screamed, "Call campus security"

    f. Dr Jamison will give his Introduction to Public Policy final exam on Wednesday

    g. When will Mrs Smith, the English instructor, return from her meeting with Dean Capers

    a. A question mark (?) is needed to end a statement beginning with *When*.

    b. A period (.) is needed after the abbreviation (*Mr.*). A period is needed to end a statement (. . . *Ohio.*).

    c. An exclamation point (!) is needed to end a statement expressing a strong emotion. (*Call 911!*). *Call 911* is a direct quotation. The exclamation point should be placed inside the quotation marks (*"Call 911!"*).

    d. A question mark (?) is needed to end a statement beginning with *Where. Where is the library* is a direct quotation. The question mark should be placed inside the quotation marks (*"Where is the library?"*).

    e. A period (.) is needed to end a statement (. . . *ajar.*). An exclamation point (!) is needed after a statement that expresses a strong emotion (*"Call campus security!"*). The exclamation point should be placed inside the quotation marks.

    f. A period (.) is needed after the abbreviation (*Dr.*). A period (.) is needed to end a statement (. . . *Wednesday.*)

    g. A period (.) is needed after the abbreviation (*Mrs.*). A question mark is needed to end a statement beginning with *When.*

# CHAPTER 14

# Internal Punctuation Marks

## 14.1 The Comma

Of all the marks of punctuation, the comma (,) has the most uses. Before you tackle the main principles that guide its usage, be sure that you have an elementary understanding of sentence structure. There are actually only a few rules and conventions to follow when using commas; the rest is common sense. The worst abuse of commas comes from those who overuse them or who place them illogically. If you are ever in doubt as to whether or not to use a comma, do not use it.

### 14.1.1 In a Series

When more than one adjective (an adjective series) describes a noun, use a comma to separate and emphasize each adjective.

the long, dark passageway

another confusing, sleepless night

an elaborate, complex plan

In these instances, the comma takes the place of "and." To test if the comma is needed, try inserting "and" between the adjectives in question. If it is logical, you should use a comma. The following are examples of adjectives that describe an adjective-noun combination that has come to be thought of almost as one word. In such cases, the adjective in front of the adjective-noun combination needs no comma.

| | |
|---|---|
| a stately *oak tree* | my worst *report card* |
| an exceptional *wine glass* | a borrowed *record player* |
| a successful *garage sale* | a porcelain *dinner plate* |

If you insert *and* between the adjectives in the above examples, it will not make sense.

The comma is also used to separate words, phrases, and whole ideas (clauses); it still takes the place of *and* when used this way.

an apple, a pear, a fig, and a banana

a lovely lady, an indecent dress, and many admirers

She lowered the shade, closed the curtain, turned off the light, and went to bed.

John, Frank, and my Uncle Harry all thought it was a questionable theory.

The only question that exists about the use of commas in a series is whether or not one should be used before the final item. Usually *and* or *or* precedes the final item, and many writers do not include the comma before the final *and* or *or*. However, it is advisable to use the comma, because often its omission can be confusing—in such cases as these, for instance.

> NO: Would you like to shop at RSVideo's, Quick Stop's and Steenbeck's Pet Store?

> YES: Would you like to shop at RSVideo's, Quick Stop's, and Steenbeck's Pet Store?

> NO: He got on his horse, tracked rabbits and deer and rode on to Canton.

> YES: He got on his horse, tracked rabbits and deer, and rode on to Canton.

> NO: We planned the trip with Mary and Harold, Susan, Dick and Joan, Gregory and Jean and Charles. (*Is it Gregory*

*and Jean or Jean and Charles or Gregory and Jean and Charles?*)

### 14.1.2 With Introductory Words, Phrases, and Clauses

Usually if a phrase or clause precedes the subject at the beginning of a sentence, a comma is used to set it off.

After last night's fiasco at the disco, she couldn't bear the thought of looking at him again. (introductory phrase)

Whenever I try to talk about politics, my husband leaves the room. (introductory clause)

If an introductory phrase includes a verb form that is being used as another part of speech (a *verbal*), it must be followed by a comma. Introductory elliptical clauses must also be followed by a comma. Try to make sense of the following sentences without commas.

NO:  When eating Mary never looked up from her plate.

YES:  When eating, Mary never looked up from her plate. (elliptical clause)

NO:  Because of her desire to follow her faith in James wavered.

YES:  Because of her desire to follow, her faith in James wavered.

Above all, common sense is the best guideline when trying to decide whether or not to use a comma after an introductory phrase. Does the comma make the meaning clearer? If it does, use it; if not, there is no reason to insert it.

### 14.1.3 To Separate Sentences with Two Main Ideas (Compound Sentences)

To understand this use of the comma, you need to have studied sentence structure and be able to recognize compound sentences.

When a sentence contains two independent clauses and the two clauses are joined by a connecting word (*and, but, or, yet, for, nor*), use a comma before the connecting word to show that another clause is coming.

I thought I knew the poem by heart, but he showed me three lines I had forgotten.

Are we really interested in helping the children, or are we more concerned with protecting our good names?

If the two parts of the sentence are short and closely related, it is not necessary to use a comma.

He threw the ball and the dog ran after it.

Jane played the piano and Charles danced.

**Errors to Avoid**

Be careful not to confuse a compound sentence with a sentence that has a compound verb and a single subject. If the subject is the same for both verbs, there is no need for a comma.

NO: Charles sent some flowers, and wrote a long letter explaining why he had not been able to come.

NO: Last Thursday we went to the concert with Julia, and afterward dined at an old Italian restaurant.

## 14.1.4 With Interrupting Material

There are so many different kinds of interruptions that can occur in a sentence that a list of them all would be quite lengthy. In general, words and phrases that stop the flow of the sentence or are unnecessary for the main idea are set off by commas.

**Abbreviations after names**

Did you invite John Paul, Jr., and his sister?

**Interjections:** An exclamation added without grammatical connection.

Oh, I'm so glad to see you.

**Direct address**

Roy, won't you open the door for the dog?

I can't understand, Mother, what you are trying to say.

**Tag questions:** A question that repeats the helping verb and is in the negative.

I'm really hungry, aren't you?

Jerry looks like his father, doesn't he?

**Geographical names and addresses**

The concert will be held in Chicago, Illinois, on August 12.

The letter was addressed to Ms. Marion Heartwell, 1881 Pine Lane, Palo Alto, California 95824. (*No comma is used before a zip code.*)

**Transitional words and phrases**

On the other hand, I hope he gets better.

You'll find, therefore, no one more loyal to you than me.

**Parenthetical words and phrases**

You will become, I believe, a great statesman.
We know, of course, that this is the only thing to do.

**Unusual word order**

The dress, new and crisp, hung in the closet. (*Normal word order: The new, crisp dress hung in the closet.*)

Intently, she stared out the window. (*Normal word order: She stared intently out the window.*)

## 14.1.5   With Nonrestrictive Elements (Not Essential to the Meaning)

Parts of a sentence that modify other parts are sometimes essential to the meaning of the sentence and sometimes not. When a modifying word or group of words is not vital to the meaning of the sentence, it is set off by commas. Since it does not restrict the meaning of the words it modifies, it is called **nonrestrictive**. Modifiers that are essential to the meaning of the sentence are called **restrictive** and are not set off by commas. Compare the following pairs of sentences:

The girl *who wrote the story* is my sister. (essential)

My sister, *the girl who wrote the story,* has always been drawn to adventure. (nonessential)

The cup *that is on the piano* is the one I want. (essential)

The cup, *which my brother gave me last year,* is on the piano. (nonessential)

She always listened to her sister *Jean.* (essential—she must have more than one sister)

She always listened to her husband, *Jack.* (nonessential—obviously, she has only one husband)

### 14.1.6 With Direct Quotations

Most direct quotations or quoted materials are set off from the rest of the sentence by commas.

"Please read your part more loudly," the director insisted.

"I won't know what to do," said Michael, "if you leave me now."

Mark looked up from his work, smiled, and said, "We'll be with you in a moment."

Be careful not to set off indirect quotations or quotations that are used as subjects or complements.

"To be or not to be" is the famous beginning of a soliloquy in Shakespeare's *Hamlet.* (subject)

Back then my favorite song was "A Summer Place" (complement)

She said she would never come back. (indirect quote)

### 14.1.7 With Contrasting Elements

Her intelligence, *not her beauty,* got her the job.

Your plan will take you farther from, *rather than closer to,* your destination.

## 14.1.8 With Dates

Both forms of the date are acceptable.

She will arrive on April 6, 2000.

He left on 5 December 2000.

No commas are necessary when only the month and year are used.

In January 2000 he handed in his resignation.

## Problem Solving Example:

Insert commas where needed in the following sentences.

a. "Your cellular telephone is ringing" said the student standing behind me in the bookstore line.

b. Today's college students bring a computer a printer and a fax machine with them to campus.

c. You will learn I believe many Internet searching tools in Dr. Brown's Information Technology class.

d. Summer semester begins Monday June 9 and ends Friday August 1.

e. Professor Scott I e-mailed you my assignment yesterday.

f. This year I am taking American literature and next year I will take British literature.

g. When telephoning the automated registration system you will need your student identification number.

h. My new job is in Los Angeles California.

i. You have checked your e-mail lately haven't you.

j. The sign on the dormitory lobby wall reads "This lobby closes at midnight."

a. "Your cellular telephone is ringing," said the student standing behind me in the bookstore line. *Your cellular telephone is ringing* is a direct quotation. A comma sets a quotation off from the rest of the sentence.

b. Today's college students bring a computer, a printer, and a fax machine with them to campus. A comma is needed after each item in a series.

c. You will learn, I believe, many Internet searching tools in Dr. Brown's Information Technology class. A comma is needed around a parenthetical expression that interrupts the flow of a sentence.

d. Summer semester begins Monday, June 9, and ends Friday, August 1. A comma is needed after the day of the week and the day of the month.

e. Professor Scott, I e-mailed you my assignment yesterday. A comma is needed after a direct address.

f. This year I am taking American literature, and next year I will take British literature. A comma is needed between two independent clauses that are joined by a coordinating conjunction.

g. When telephoning the automated registration system, you will need your student identification number. A comma is needed after an introductory subordinate clause beginning a sentence.

h. My new job is in Los Angeles, California. A comma is needed between a city and a state.

i. You have checked your e-mail lately, haven't you. A comma precedes the negative portion of a tag question.

j. The sign on the dormitory lobby wall reads, "This lobby closes at midnight." A comma is needed to set off the quotation.

## 14.2   The Semicolon

The **semicolon** (;) is sometimes called a mild period. It indicates a pause midway in length between the comma and the colon. Writing that contains many semicolons is usually in a dignified, formal style. To use them correctly, it is necessary to be able to recognize main clauses—complete ideas. When two main clauses occur in a single sentence without a connecting word (*and, but, or, nor, for*), the appropriate mark of punctuation is the semicolon.

It is not a good idea for you to leave the country right now; you should actually try to stay as long as you possibly can.

In the past, boy babies were often dressed in blue; girls, in pink. (*"Were often dressed" is understood in the second part of the sentence.*)

Burgundy and maroon are very similar colors; scarlet is altogether different.

Notice how the use of the comma, period, and semicolon gives a sentence a slightly different meaning.

Music lightens life; literature deepens it.

Just as music lightens life, literature deepens it.

Music lightens life. Literature deepens it.

The semicolon lends a certain balance to writing that would otherwise be difficult to achieve. Nonetheless, you should be careful not to overuse it. A comma can just as well join parts of a sentence with two main ideas; the semicolon is particularly appropriate if there is a striking contrast in the two ideas expressed.

Ask not what your country can do for you; ask what you can do for your country.

It started out as an ordinary day; it ended being the most extraordinary of her life.

If any one of the following conjunctive adverbs, words, or phrases is used to join compound sentences, it is preceded by a semicolon and is usually followed by a comma.

| | | | |
|---|---|---|---|
| then | however | thus | furthermore |
| hence | indeed | consequently | also |
| that is | nevertheless | anyhow | in addition |
| in fact | on the other hand | likewise | moreover |
| still | meanwhile | instead | besides |
| otherwise | in other words | henceforth | for example |
| therefore | at the same time | even now | nonetheless |

For a long time, people thought that women were inferior to men; *even now*, it is not an easy attitude to overcome.

Being clever and cynical, he succeeded in becoming president of the company; *meanwhile*, his wife left him.

Cigarette smoking has never interested me; *furthermore*, I couldn't care less if anyone else smokes or not.

When a series of complicated items is listed or when there is internal punctuation in a series, the semicolon is sometimes used to make the meaning clearer.

You can use your new car for many things: to drive to town or to the country; to impress your friends and neighbors; to protect yourself from rain on a trip away from home; and to borrow against should you need money right away.

The scores from yesterday's games came in last night: Pirates-6, Zoomers-3; Caterpillars-12, Steelys-8; Crashers-9, Links-8; and Greens-15, Uptowns-4.

The semicolon is placed outside quotation marks or parentheses, unless it is a part of the material enclosed in those marks.

I used to call him "my lord and master"; it made him laugh every time.

The weather was cold for that time of year (I was shivering wherever I went); nevertheless, we set out to hike to the top of that mountain.

## Problem Solving Example:

Punctuate the following sentences using the semicolon.

a. Patrick thought the problem was solved instead, his solution proved entirely wrong.

b. I want to study pre-med therefore, I must take chemistry and biology.

c. My professors are Dr. Harris English Dr. Wilkes history Dr. Green sociology and Dr. Witham physical education.

d. I must complete my term paper it is due tomorrow.

a. Patrick thought the problem was solved; instead, his solution proved entirely wrong. *Instead* joins two independent clauses. A semicolon precedes *instead*, and a comma follows it.

b. I want to study pre-med; therefore, I must take chemistry and biology. *Therefore* is a conjunctive adverb that joins two independent clauses. A semicolon precedes *therefore*, and a comma follows it.

c. My professors are Dr. Harris, English; Dr. Wilkes, history; Dr. Green, sociology; and Dr. Whitham, physical education. A semicolon joins items in a series if there are commas within each item. In this sentence, the professor's name is followed by the department name. A comma is placed after the professor's name and a semicolon is placed after the department's name.

d. I must complete my term paper; it is due tomorrow. A semicolon joins two independent clauses without a conjunction.

## 14.3 The Colon

**The colon** (:) is the sign of a pause about midway in length between the semicolon and the period. It can often be replaced by a comma and sometimes by a period. Although used less frequently now than it was 50 to 75 years ago, the colon is still convenient to use, for it signals to the reader that more information is to come on the subject of concern. The colon can also create a slight dramatic tension.

It is used to introduce a word, a phrase, or a complete statement (clause) that emphasizes, illustrates, or exemplifies what has already been stated.

He had only one desire in life: to play baseball.

The weather that day was the most unusual I'd ever seen: it snowed and rained while the sun was still shining.

Since the colon is not an end mark (used to end a sentence), do not capitalize after the colon unless the word is a proper noun.

May I offer you a suggestion: don't drive without your seat belts fastened.

The thought continued to perplex him: where will I go next?

When introducing a series that illustrates or emphasizes what has already been stated, use the colon.

Only a few of the graduates were able to be there: Jamison, Mearns, Linkley, and Commoner.

For Omar Khayam, a Persian poet, three things are necessary for a paradise on earth: a loaf of bread, a jug of wine, and one's beloved.

Long quotations set off from the rest of the text by indentation rather than quotation marks are generally introduced with a colon.

The first line of Lincoln's Gettysburg address is familiar to most Americans:

Fourscore and seven years ago our fathers brought forth on this continent a new nation, conceived in liberty and dedicated to the proposition that all men are created equal.

I quote from Shakespeare's *Sonnets*:

When I do count the clock that tells the time,
And see the brave day sunk in hideous night;
When I behold the violet past prime,
And sable curls all silver's o'er with white. . .

It is also customary to begin a business letter with a colon.

Dear Senator Jordan:

Dear Manager:

Gentlemen:

Dear Sir or Madam:

In informal letters use a comma.

Dear Mary,

Dear Father,

The colon is also used in introducing a list.

Please send the following:
1.  50 index cards
2.  4 typewriter ribbons
3.  8 erasers

Prepare the recipe as follows:
1.  Slice the oranges thinly.
2.  Arrange them in a circle around the strawberries.
3.  Pour the liqueur over both fruits.

At least three ladies will have to be there to help:
1.  Mrs. Goldman, who will greet the guests;
2.  Harriet Sacher, who will serve the lunch; and
3.  my sister, who will do whatever else needs to be done.

Do not use a colon after a linking verb or a preposition.

> NO: My favorite holidays are: Christmas, Halloween, and New Year's Eve.

> YES: My favorite holidays are Christmas, Halloween, and New Year's Eve.

Finally, the colon is used between numbers when writing the time, between the volume and number of volume and page number of a journal, and between the chapter and verse in the Bible.

4:30 P.M.

The Nation, 34:8

Genesis 5:18

## Problem Solving Example:

Place a colon where needed in the following items.

a.  The teacher asked the students to bring the following items to class

1. textbook

2. paper

3. pen

b.  Dear President Clinton

    c.  The reference citation read, *Journal of School Research 9 2.*

    d.  For Internet access, a person needs three things an Internet service provider, a computer, and a modem.

    a.  The teacher asked the students to bring the following items to class:

       1. textbook

       2. paper

       3. pen

A colon is needed to introduce a list.

    b.  Dear President Clinton:

A colon is needed to begin a business letter.

    c.  The reference citation read, *Journal of School Research 9:2.* A colon is needed between the volume and the number of a journal.

    d.  For Internet access, a person needs three things: an Internet service provider, a computer, and a modem. A colon is needed to introduce a list (*an Internet service provider, a computer, and a modem*).

## 14.4 The Dash

Use the **dash** (—) to indicate a sudden or unexpected break in the normal flow of the sentence. It can also be used in place of parentheses or of commas if the meaning is clarified. Usually the dash gives special emphasis to the material it sets off. On a typewriter, two hyphens (--) indicate a dash.

Could you—I hate to ask!—help me with these boxes?

When we left town—a day never to be forgotten—they had a record snowfall.

She said—we all heard it—"The safe is not locked."

A dash is often used to summarize a series of ideas that have already been expressed.

Freedom of speech, freedom to vote and freedom of assembly—these are the cornerstones of democracy.

Carbohydrates, fats, and proteins—these are the basic kinds of food we need.

The dash is also used to note the author of a quotation that is set off in the text.

*Nothing is good or bad but thinking makes it so.*
—William Shakespeare

## 14.5   Parentheses

To set off material that is only loosely connected to the central meaning of the sentence, use **parentheses** [( )].

Most women (at least, most that I know) like wine, men, and song but have too much work and not enough time for such enjoyments.

On Tuesday evenings and Thursday afternoons (the times I don't have classes), the television programs are not too exciting.

Watch out for other punctuation when you use parentheses. Punctuation that refers to the material enclosed in the parentheses occurs inside the marks. Punctuation belonging to the rest of the sentence comes outside the parentheses.

I thought I knew the poem by heart (boy, was I wrong!).

For a long time (too long as far as I'm concerned), women were thought to be inferior to men.

We must always strive to tell the truth. (Are we even sure we know what truth is?)

When I first saw a rose (don't you think it's the most beautiful flower?), I thought it must be man-made.

## 14.6    Quotation Marks

The proper use of **quotation marks** must be studied and learned, because some of their uses appear arbitrary and outside common sense.

The most common use of double quotation marks (" ") is to set off quoted words, phrases, and sentences.

> *"If everybody minded their own business," said the duchess in a hoarse growl, "the world would go round a great deal faster than it does."*
>
> *"Then you would say what you mean," the March Hare went on.*
>
> *"I do," Alice hastily replied: "At least—at least I mean what I say— that's the same thing, you know."*
>
> *"Not the same thing a bit!" said the Hatter. "Why, you might just as well say that 'I see what I eat' is the same thing as 'I eat what I see'!"*
>
> Both quotations from Lewis Carroll's
> *Alice in Wonderland*

In the latter quotation, single quotation marks are used to set off quoted material within a quotation. Other examples of correct use of single quotation marks:

> "Shall I bring 'Rime of the Ancient Mariner' along with us?" she asked her brother.
>
> Mrs. Green said, "The doctor told me, 'Go immediately to bed when you get home.'"

### 14.6.1    With Commas and Periods

Remember that commas and periods are always placed inside quotation marks even if they are not actually part of the quote.

> NO:    "Get down here right away", John cried. "You'll miss the sunset if you don't".
>
> YES:    "Get down here right away," John cried. "You'll miss the sunset if you don't."

> NO: "If my dog could talk", Mary mused, "I'll bet he would say 'Take me for a walk right this minute.'"
>
> YES: "If my dog could talk," Mary mused, "I'll bet he would say 'Take me for a walk right this minute.'"

### 14.6.2 With Question Marks and Exclamation Points

Other marks of punctuation, such as question marks, exclamation points, colons, and semicolons, go inside the quotation marks if they are part of the quoted material. If they are not part of the quote, however, they go outside the quotation marks. Be careful to distinguish between the guidelines for the comma and period, which *always* go inside the quotation marks, and those for the other marks of punctuation.

> NO: Did you hear her say, "He'll be there early?" (*The question mark belongs to the entire sentence and not to the quote alone.*)
>
> YES: Did you hear her say, "He'll be there early"?
>
> NO: She called down the stairs, "When are you coming"? (*The question marks belongs to the quote*)
>
> YES: She called down the stairs, "When are you coming?"
>
> NO: "Ask not what your country can do for you," said Kennedy; "ask what you can do for your country:" a statement of genius I think. (*Semicolons and colons are always placed outside closing quotation marks.*)
>
> YES: "Ask not what your country can do for you," said Kennedy; "ask what you can do for your country": a statement of genius, I think.
>
> NO: "Let me out"! he cried. "Don't you have any pity"?
>
> YES: "Let me out!" he cried. "Don't you have any pity?"

Remember to use only one mark of punctuation at the end of a sentence ending with a quotation.

> NO: She thought aloud, "Will I ever finish this paper in time for that class?".
>
> YES: She thought aloud, "Will I ever finish this paper in time for that class?"

NO:    "Not the same thing a bit!", said the Hatter. "Why, you might just as well say that 'I see what I eat' is the same thing as 'I eat what I see'!".

YES:   "Not the same thing a bit!" said the Hatter. "Why, you might just as well say that 'I see what I eat' is the same thing as 'I eat what I see'!"

### 14.6.3 Writing Dialogue

When writing dialogue, begin a new paragraph each time the speaker changes.

"Do you know what time it is?" asked Jane. "I don't want to be late for my class."

"Can't you see I'm busy?" snapped Mary. "Go into the kitchen if you want the time."

"It's easy to see you're in a bad mood today," replied Jane.

Use quotation marks to enclose words used as words. Sometimes italics are used for this purpose.

"Judgment" had always been a difficult word for me to spell.

I always thought "nice" meant "particular" or "having exacting standards," but I know now it has acquired a much more general and vague meaning.

If slang is used within more formal writing, the slang words or phrases should be set off with quotation marks.

The "good old boy" system is responsible for most promotions in today's corporate world.

Harrison's decision to leave the conference and to "stick his neck out" by flying to Jamaica was applauded by the rest of the participants.

When words are meant to have an unusual or special significance to the reader, for instance irony or humor, they are sometimes placed in quotation marks. This is, however, a practice to be avoided whenever possible. The reader should be able to get the intended meaning from the context.

For years, women were not allowed to buy real estate in order to "protect" them from unscrupulous dealers. (*The writer is using somebody else's word; the use of the quotation marks shows he or she does not believe women needed protection.*)

The "conversation" resulted in one black eye and a broken arm.

To set off titles of TV show episodes, poems, stories, newspaper and magazine articles, and chapters in a book, use quotation marks. (Book, motion picture, radio and TV show, newspaper, and magazine titles are underlined.)

The article "Moving South in the Southern Rain," by Jergen Smith in the *Southern News*, attracted the attention of our editor.

My favorite essay by Montaigne is "On Silence."

You will find Keats' "Ode on a Grecian Urn" in Chapter 3, "The Romantic Era," in Lastly's *Selections from Great English Poets*.

**Errors to Avoid**

Be sure to remember that quotation marks always come in pairs. Do not make the mistake of using only one set.

NO: "You'll never convince me to move to the city, said Thurman. I consider it an insane asylum."

YES: "You'll never convince me to move to the city," said Thurman. "I consider it an insane asylum."

When a quotation consists of several sentences, do not put the quotation marks at the beginning and the end of each sentence; put them at the beginning and end of the entire quotation.

NO: "It was during his student days in Bonn that Beethoven fastened upon Schiller's poem." "The heady sense of liberation in the verses must have appealed to him." "They appealed to every German."

—John Burke

YES: "It was during his student days in Bonn that Beethoven fastened upon Schiller's poem. The heady sense of liberation in the verses must have appealed to him. They appealed to every German."

—John Burke

Instead of setting off a long quotation with quotation marks, you may want to indent and single space it. If you do indent, do not use quotation marks.

> We are not enemies, but friends. We must not be enemies. Though passion may have strained, it must not break, our bonds of affection. The mystic chords of memory, stretching from every battlefield and patriot grave to every living heart and hearthstone all over the broad land, will yet swell the chorus of the Union when again touched, as surely they will be, by the better angels of our nature.
> —Abraham Lincoln, First Inaugural Address

Be careful not to use quotation marks with indirect quotations.

NO: Mary wondered "if she would ever get over it."

YES: Mary wondered if she would ever get over it.

NO: "My exercise teacher told me," Mary said, "'that I should do these back exercises 15 minutes each day.'"

YES: "My exercise teacher told me," Mary said, "that I should do these back exercises 15 minutes each day."

When you quote several paragraphs, it is not sufficient to place quotation marks at the beginning and end of the entire quote. Place quotation marks *at the beginning of each paragraph, but at the end of only the last paragraph.* Here is an abbreviated quotation for an example.

"Here begins an odyssey through the world of classical mythology, starting with the creation of the world, proceeding to the divinities that once governed all aspects of human life.

"It is true that themes similar to the classical may be found in almost any corpus of mythology. Each technology is not immune to the influence of Greece and Rome.

"We hardly need mention the extent to which painters and sculptors have used and adapted classical mythology to illustrate the past, to reveal the human body, to express romantic or antiromantic ideals, or to symbolize any particular point of view."

## Problem Solving Example:

Punctuate the following sentences correctly using quotation marks.

a. My favorite *ER* episode was And Then There Were None.

b. Professor Williams, I won't be late to your class again said the student.

c. Tom, Professor Williams replied at this college, three tardies equal one absence.

d. I enjoy reading Julian Smith's column Campus Today in the college's newspaper.

e. My psychology professor is having the class read The Effect of Panic Disorder on High School Students in *Psychology Journal*.

a. My favorite *ER* episode was "And Then There Were None." Quotation marks are placed around the title of a television show's episode.

b. "Professor Williams, I won't be late to your class again," said the student. Quotation marks are needed around the speaker's words. A comma is needed to set off the quotation from the remainder of the sentence.

c. "Tom," Professor Williams replied, "at this college, three tardies equal one absence." Quotation marks are needed around the speaker's words. A comma is needed to set off each part of the quotation from the remainder of the sentence.

d. I enjoy reading Julian Smith's column "Campus Today" in the college's newspaper. Quotation marks are needed around the name of the newspaper column.

e. My psychology professor is having the class read "The Effect of Panic Disorder on High School Students" in *Psychology Journal*. Quotation marks are placed around the title of a journal article.

## 14.7 The Apostrophe

### 14.7.1 To Indicate Omission

Use the **apostrophe** to form contractions and to indicate that letters or figures have been omitted.

| | |
|---|---|
| can't (cannot) | o'clock (of the clock) |
| I'll (I will) | it's (it is) |
| memories of '42 (1942) | won't (will not) |
| You've (you have) | they're (they are) |

Notice that the apostrophe is always placed where a letter or letters have been omitted. Avoid such careless errors as writing *wo'nt* instead of *won't*, for example. Contractions are generally not used in formal writing. They are found primarily in speech and informal writing.

### 14.7.2 To Indicate the Plural Form

An apostrophe is also used to indicate the plural form of letters, figures, and words that normally don't take a plural form. In such cases it might be confusing to add only an "s."

He quickly learned his *r*'s and *s*'s.

Most of the *Ph.D.'s* and *M.D.'s* understand the new technology they are using for anticancer drugs.

Her *2*'s always looked like her *4*'s.

Marion used too many *the's* and *and's* in her last paper for English literature.

Whenever possible, try to form plurals by adding only "s" to numbers and to single or multiple letters used as words.

| | |
|---|---|
| the ABCs | the 1940s |
| in threes and fours | three Rs |

### 14.7.3 To Indicate Possession

In spoken English, the same pronunciation is used for the plural, singular possessive, and plural possessive of most nouns. It is only in context that the listener is able to tell the difference in the words used by the speaker. In written English, spelling as well as context tells readers the meaning of the noun the writer is using. The writer has only to master the placement of the apostrophe so that the meaning is clearly conveyed to the reader. These words are pronounced alike but have different meanings.

| PLURAL | SINGULAR POSSESSIVE | PLURAL POSSESSIVE |
|---|---|---|
| neighbors | neighbor's | neighbors' |
| doctors | doctor's | doctors' |
| weeks | week's | weeks' |
| sopranos | soprano's | sopranos' |
| civilizations | civilization's | civilizations' |
| bosses | boss's | bosses' |

If you aren't sure of the apostrophe's placement, you can determine it accurately by this simple test: change the possessive phrase into "belonging to" or into an "of" phrase to discover the basic noun. You will find this a particularly useful trick for some of the more confusing possessive forms, such as those on words that end in "s' or "es."

Keats' poem: The poem belonging to Keats. Base noun is *Keats*; possessive is Keats' or Keats's, not Keat's or Keatsies.

The Joneses' house: The house of the Joneses (plural of Jones). Base is *Joneses*; possessive is Joneses', not Jones' or Jones'es.

Four months' pay: The pay of four months. *Months* is base; possessive is months', not month's.

The lioness' strength: The strength of the lioness. *Lioness* is base; possessive is lioness' or lioness's, not lioness'es or liones's.

It is anybody's guess: The guess of anybody. *Anybody* is the base noun; possessive is anybody's, not anybodys' or anybodies'.

## Problem Solving Example:

 Correct any errors in apostrophe use in the following sentences.

    a. I cant find my student identification card.

b. The Department of English graduated 28 B.A.s, 10 M.A.s, and 2 Ph.D.s this spring.

c. Joes history term paper is due on Thursday.

d. Two students projects are about helping the homeless build self-esteem.

e. I told the dormitory housekeeper that the womens restroom in the lobby needs to be cleaned.

a. An apostrophe is needed to indicate the omitted letter *o* in the contraction for *cannot* (can't).

b. An apostrophe is needed to form the plural of letters (*28 B.A.'s, 10 M.A.'s,* and *2 Ph.D.'s*). Note: These may also be written BA's, MA's, PhD's; or BAs MAs, and PhDs.

c. An apostrophe and an *–s* is needed to show possession of the proper noun *Joe* (Joe's).

d. An apostrophe is placed after the *–s* on *students* (students') to indicate plural possession: *the projects of two students.*

e. The word *women* is irregular plural. To make an irregular plural possessive, add an apostrophe and an *–s* (women's).

## 14.8 Italics

**Italic** is a particular kind of type used by printers. It is a light, thin type that slants to the right. In writing or typing, italic is indicated by underlining. Although its usage varies a great deal, there are some general guidelines that should be followed.

Italics are used most often to indicate the title of a play, book, television or radio program, movie, long poem, newspaper, magazine, musical composition, work of art, ship, train, or aircraft.

She had just read Kenneth Clark's *Civilization.*

Leonardo da Vinci's most famous painting must certainly be *La Gioconda* which we know as the Mona Lisa. (Traditional titles or nicknames are not underlined.)

The *New York Times* (or New York *Times*) may be the best paper in the world. (The name of the city associated with a newspaper and

considered part of the title may or may not be italicized.)
The *Enola Gay* dropped the first atomic bomb on Hiroshima.

Note: When the overall text is italicized (as in the sentence below), the work that would otherwise be italicized should be in Roman (straight) type to better indicate the contrast.

*The* Enola Gay *dropped the first atomic bomb on Hiroshima.*

## Errors to Avoid

Reserve the use of quotation marks for short parts of longer works, such as stories, poems, and chapters, and for the titles of episodes of radio and TV shows. This helps distinguish the title of a book from a chapter, the name of an article from a magazine title, a poem from the collection in which it appears, and an episode from a TV show.

NO: *The Southern Predicament* that ran in the *Atlantic Monthly* in February received attention from us all.

YES: "The Southern Predicament" that ran in the *Atlantic Monthly* in February received attention from us all.

NO: Chapter 6, *The Marijuana Question,* seems to me the most controversial part of *Drugs Today* by Himmel.

YES: Chapter 6, "The Marijuana Question," seems to me the most controversial part of *Drugs Today* by Himmel.

Use italics to indicate a foreign word that has not yet become part of accepted English. Refer to your dictionary in order to be sure of the status of a particular word. Examples of familiar foreign words that are already part of our language and that should not be italicized are

| | | |
|---|---|---|
| a priori | psyche | status quo |
| cliché | élan | ad hoc |
| staccato | trattoria | andante |
| fait accompli | ipso facto | rendezvous |
| tête-à-tête | dolce vita | au pair |

Some foreign phrases and words that should be italicized are:

The Perellis all called "*arrivederci*," as Daniel left. (Italian for "farewell")

She'd always had a *femme de chambre*. (French for "chambermaid")

When words are referred to as words, then either quotation marks or italics can be used. (See *Quotation Marks*)

> I'm never sure whether to use "infer" or "imply."
> > OR
>
> I'm never sure whether to use *infer* or *imply*.

> My "2s" and "4s" look similar.
> > OR
>
> My *2*'s and *4*'s look similar.

Sometimes special emphasis is put on a word or phrase by underlining, italicizing, or placing it in quotation marks. Minimize this practice whenever you can; try to indicate emphasis by word order or syntax, rather than by excessive underlining, which reflects laziness on the part of the writer.

> She didn't ask John to come; she asked *me*.

> It's *time* that heals our wounds.

## 14.9  Hyphens

### 14.9.1  Compound Words

There are literally hundreds of rules for the use of **hyphens**—especially in compound words. The following are some of the most important, more dependable rules for hyphenation of compounds.

Hyphenate two or more words used as adjectives when you want to express the idea of a unit, if they come before the word they modify. If, however, they follow the main word, they should generally not be hyphenated. (See *Adjectives and Adverbs*.)

| | |
|---|---|
| well-known man | a man who is well known |
| twelve-foot ceiling | a ceiling of twelve feet |
| up-to-date information | he is up to date |
| on-the-job training | training is on the job |

There are exceptions. Some compound adjectives retain the hyphen even if they follow the word they modify. Here are some you should know:

All words (nouns and adjectives) that start with *self*:

| | |
|---|---|
| self-reliant boy | he is self-reliant |
| self-supporting girl | she is self-supporting |
| self-cleaning oven | it is self-cleaning |

All adjective compounds that start with *all*:

| | |
|---|---|
| all-encompassing book | the book is all-encompassing |

All adjectival compounds that start with *half*:

| | |
|---|---|
| half-done cake | cake was half-done |
| half-awake student | student was half-awake |
| half-explored territory | territory is only half-explored |

Compound adjectives that use *ly* are not hyphenated before or after the word they modify.

| | |
|---|---|
| highly developed muscles | his muscles were highly developed |
| interestingly formed rocks | rocks that are interestingly formed |

In general, compound words that serve as nouns are not hyphenated. Compare:

*Problem solving* (noun) was his talent.

He had a *problem-solving* (adjective) talent.

Mary is a *foster child*. (noun)

She lives at the *foster-child* (adjective) home.

## 14.9.2 Exceptions

All *in-laws* take a hyphen.

| | | |
|---|---|---|
| brother-in-law | mother-in-law | sisters-in-law |

In addition, hyphens have other uses, as follows:

In a series of hyphenated words with a common ending, hyphens are carried over so it is not necessary to repeat the word each time.

Is it a 100- or 200-page book?

Do you want a two-, three-, or five-column page?

They took six- and eight-cylinder cars along.

Both pro- and anti-American sentiment mounted.

Numbers from 21 to 99 are hyphenated when they are spelled out.

eighty-eight

sixty-three

two hundred forty-four

A hyphen is used to mean "up to and including" when used between numbers and dates

1965-75                                    There will be 10-15 people.

The academic year 1992-93

A hyphen is also used to avoid ambiguity when two capitalized names stand together.

the Boston-New York game

the Chicago-London flight

the Kramer-Lewis debate

the Harrison-Jones marriage

Many words still have prefixes that are set off by hyphens.

pre-engineering                    ex-wife (*always set "ex" off*)

pro-German                         semi-independent

anti-Nixon (*prefixes added to proper nouns should always be hyphenated*)

## 14.10 Brackets

**Brackets** are probably the least used form of the pause. They do, however, serve some very useful purposes in clarifying material. When an editor needs to add corrections, explanations, or comments, brackets are used.

"They [the Murphys] never meant to send that message to the White House." (Without the bracketed words, the reader would not know who had sent the message.)

Morris continued, "After the treaty was signed [The Treaty of Versailles], jubilation filled their hearts."

The *Times* printed the senator's speech, which was addressed to "my countrymen, my countywomen [sic]." (The term [sic] indicates that the error is in the original source quoted; in this case "countywomen" should have been "countrywomen."

Brackets are also used to avoid confusion when it is necessary to use parentheses inside of parentheses.

Darkness fell so rapidly that she and her companion (June Morrison, who had herself traveled throughout Africa [particularly Nigeria]) hardly noticed the transition from crystal blue to black.

We know of a number of scholars who disagree with this theory (see Jackson Hewitt, *To Earth's Center* [Boston: Inkwell Press, 1953], p. 614).

## 14.11 Ellipsis

**Ellipsis** points are dots used to show that a word, phrase, line, or paragraph has been omitted. Three dots indicate an omission within a sentence or between the first and last words of a quoted fragment of a sentence. Four dots (a period followed by three dots) indicate the following: the last part of the quoted sentence; the first part of the next sentence; a whole sentence or more; or a whole paragraph or more. If the original sentence ends with an exclamation point or a question mark, the punctuation mark remains followed by three ellipsis points.

"Fourscore and seven years ago, our fathers brought forth upon this continent a new nation, . . ."

"I pledge allegiance to the flag of the United States of America . . . one nation under God . . ."

## Quiz: End Punctuation Marks and Internal Punctuation Marks

**DIRECTIONS:** Choose the correct option.

1. Indianola, <u>Mississippi, where B. B. King and my father grew up,</u> has a population of less than 50,000 people.

   (A) Mississippi where, B.B. King and my father grew up,

   (B) Mississippi where B.B. King and my father grew up,

   (C) Mississippi; where B B. King and my father grew up,

   (D) No change is necessary.

2. John Steinbeck's best known novel *The Grapes of Wrath* is the story of the <u>Joads an Oklahoma family</u> who were driven from their dust-bowl farm and forced to become migrant workers in California.

   (A) Joads, an Oklahoma family

   (B) Joads, an Oklahoma family,

   (C) Joads; an Oklahoma family

   (D) No change is necessary.

3. All students who are interested in student teaching next <u>semester, must submit an application to the Teacher Education Office</u>.

   (A) semester must submit an application to the Teacher Education Office.

   (B) semester, must submit an application, to the Teacher Education Office.

   (C) semester: must submit an application to the Teacher Education Office.

   (D) No change is necessary.

4. Whenever you travel by <u>car, or plane, you</u> must wear a seat belt.

   (A) car or plane you

   (B) car, or plane you

   (C) car or plane, you

   (D) No change is necessary.

5. Wearing a seat belt is not just a good <u>idea, it's</u> the law.

   (A) idea; it's

   (B) idea it's.

   (C) idea. It's

   (D) No change is necessary

6. Senators and representatives can be reelected <u>indefinitely; a</u> president can only serve two terms.

   (A) indefinitely but a

   (B) indefinitely, a

   (C) indefinitely a

   (D) No change is necessary.

7. Students must pay a penalty for overdue library books, however, there is a grace period.

   (A) books; however, there

   (B) books however, there

   (C) books: however, there

   (D) No change is necessary.

8. Among the states that seceded from the Union to join the Confederacy in 1860-1861 <u>were:</u> Mississippi, Florida, and Alabama.

   (A) were

   (B) were;

(C) were.

(D) No change is necessary.

9. The art exhibit displayed works by many famous <u>artists such as:</u> Dali, Picasso, and Michelangelo.

(A) artists such as;

(B) artists such as

(C) artists. Such as

(D) No change is necessary.

10. The National Shakespeare Company will perform <u>the following plays:</u> *Othello*, *Macbeth*, *Hamlet*, and *As You Like It*.

(A) the following plays,

(B) the following plays;

(C) the following plays

(D) No change is necessary.

## ANSWER KEY

| | |
|---|---|
| 1. (D) | 6. (D) |
| 2. (B) | 7. (A) |
| 3. (A) | 8. (A) |
| 4. (C) | 9. (B) |
| 5. (A) | 10. (D) |

**CHAPTER 15**

# Numbers

## 15.1 Over 100 and Under 100

In writing, numbers can be either spelled out or represented by the figures themselves. Although there is no definite rule, there are some guidelines that should be followed.

Most writers spell out numbers under 100 and use figures for 100 and over.

| | |
|---|---|
| for eighteen years | 306 buildings |
| eleven states | only 514 more cars |
| forty-five years old | 4,762 students |
| ninety-nine percent | I agree 100 percent |

### 15.1.1 Starting a Sentence

A number that starts a sentence should always be spelled out, even if it is over 100.

Three thousand forty-two voters selected Ross.

Ninety-five dollars did not seem like much to me for the hat.

### 15.1.2 In the Same Paragraph

Within the same paragraph, numbers that refer to the same category should be treated alike. Be consistent; be careful not to use figures for some and then spell others out.

> *Forty-six men* and *118 women* joined the club last year. In comparison, the year before, *35 men* and *56 women* joined. (Only the number that starts the sentence is spelled out.)

### 15.1.3 Large Rounded Numbers

Very large numbers are usually spelled out if they are round numbers.

The earth may be 4 *billion* years old.

That house supposedly sold for $1 *million*. (Do not use both "$" and "dollars," because they mean the same thing.)

Some baseball players make $2.5 *million* a year now.

OR

Some baseball players make 2.5 *million* dollars a year now.

## 15.2 Ordinal Numbers and Fractions

Write out ordinal numbers (*fourth*, *twenty-third*, etc.) rather than writing them as figures with letter endings.

It is usually clearer to use figures when writing a fraction.

The brochure was printed on 9-inch by $12^1/_2$-inch paper.

The board for the bed was .78 of an inch too short.

When Susan was in school, she had a 3.2 average.

## 15.3 Addresses

Addresses are usually written in figures.

14 Mill Brook Road, Sumerset Glen, IA 23567

P.O. Box 583, Winding Ridge, Gloryville, WV 25432

200 East 50th Street, New York, NY 10022

When the numbers in the address can be spelled out in one or two words, it is also acceptable to spell them out.

One Park Avenue

Two Hundred West Lake Drive

Forty-one Fifth Avenue

Three Thousand Oaks Road

## 15.4 Dates

There are a number of different ways to write dates.

| | | |
|---|---|---|
| July 3, 1992 | OR | 3 July 1992 |
| July third | OR | the third of July |
| nineteenth century | OR | the 1800s |
| the sixties | OR | the '60s |

## 15.5 Parts of a Book

Whenever mentioning parts of a book (page numbers, sections, chapters, exercises), use figures.

Please refer to page 184 in chapter 6 of your history book if you want the answer to your question.

We found four case studies in section 8 of Jack's first-year law book.

The teacher assigned exercise 12 on page 235.

## 15.6 Plural Forms

To form the plural of spelled-out numbers, follow the same rules you follow to form the plural of other nouns.

They came in twos and threes.

He's in his thirties.

To form the plural of figures, add only "s."

The 1880s and the 1890s were exciting times in American history.

## Problem Solving Example:

 Proofread the following sentences for errors in expression of numbers. Correct any errors above the line.

  a. We expected 329 members to attend the 3rd annual convention.

  b. During the past 10 years, I have moved 22 times.

  c. Paula won $2,000,000 as 1st prize in the lottery.

  d. The revolutions of the 1840s were a turning point in 19th century European history.

  e. 1,139 students attended the rally in front of the administration building about the proposed 10 percent tuition increase.

 a. third. Ordinal numbers are spelled out.

  b. ten, twenty-two. Numbers under 100 are spelled out.

  c. $2 million, first. Large numbers are spelled out. Ordinal numbers are spelled out.

  d. nineteenth. Ordinal numbers are spelled out.

  e. One thousand one hundred and thirty-nine. Numbers that begin a sentence are spelled out.

# CHAPTER 16

# Capitalization

## 16.1 Proper Nouns

When a letter is capitalized, it calls special attention to itself. This attention should be for a good reason. There are standard uses for capital letters as well as much difference of opinion as to what should and should not be capitalized. In general, capitalize (1) all proper nouns, (2) the first word of a sentence, and (3) the first word of a direct quotation.

All proper nouns should be capitalized. The groups below illustrate the different classifications of words that would be capitalized.

### 16.1.1 Names of Ships, Aircraft, Spacecraft, and Trains

| | |
|---|---|
| *Apollo 13* | *Mariner IV* |
| DC-10 | *S.S. United States* |
| *Sputnik II* | Boeing 707 |

### 16.1.2 Names of Deities

| | |
|---|---|
| God | Jupiter |
| Allah | Holy Ghost |
| Buddha | Diana |
| Jehovah | Shiva |

### 16.1.3 Geological Periods

Neolithic Age              Cenozoic era

Ice Age                    Tertiary period

### 16.1.4 Names of Astronomical Bodies

Venus                      Big Dipper

the Milky Way              Halley's comet

Ursa Major                 North Star

Scorpio                    Deneb

the Crab nebula            Pleiades

(Note that *sun*, *moon*, and *earth* are not capitalized unless they are used with other astronomical terms that are capitalized.)

### 16.1.5 Personifications

Reliable *Nature* brought her promise of spring.

Bring on *Melancholy* in his sad might.

*Morning* in the bowl of night has flung the stone/That set the stars to flight.

### 16.1.6 Historical Periods

the Middle Ages            World War I

Reign of Terror            Great Depression

Christian Era              Roaring Twenties

Age of Louis XIV           Renaissance

### 16.1.7 Organizations, Associations, and Institutions

Girls Scouts of America    American Athletic Union

New York Yankees           Kiwanis Club

Smithsonian Institution    League of Women Voters

## 16.1.8 Geographic regions

The North
Southern cooking
    BUT
south of the border

## 16.1.9 Government and Judicial Groups

| | |
|---|---|
| New Jersey City Council | House of Commons |
| U.S. Senate | Parliament |
| Arkansas Supreme Court | House of Representatives |

## 16.1.10 General Terms that Accompany Specific Names

A general term that accompanies a specific name is capitalized only if it follows the specific name. If it stands alone or comes before the word, it is put in lower case.

| | |
|---|---|
| Washington State | the state of Washington |
| Senator Dirksen | the senator from Illinois |
| Central Park | the park |
| Golden Gate Bridge | the bridge |
| President Andrew Jackson | the president of the United States or the President of the United States |

## 16.1.11 Specific Versus General Names of Courses

| | |
|---|---|
| Business Calculus | calculus |
| Political Institutions | civics |
| Linguistics | English (languages are always capitalized) |
| Computer Technology | science |
| Geometry I | geometry |

## 16.2 Sentences and Sentence Fragments

Use a capital to start a sentence or a sentence fragment.

Our car would not start.

When will you leave? I need to know right away.

Never!

Let me in! Right now!

## 16.3 Sentences within Sentences

When a sentence appears within a sentence, start it with a capital.

The main question is, Where do we start?

My sister said, "I'll find the Monopoly set."

He answered, "We can stay only a few minutes."

## 16.4 Lines of Poetry

In poetry, it is usual practice to capitalize the first word of each line, even if the word comes in the middle of a sentence.

She dwells with Beauty—Beauty that must die;
And Joy, whose hand is ever at his lips
Bidding Adieu.

—John Keats *16.12*

## 16.5 Titles of Works

The most important words of titles are capitalized. Those words not capitalized are conjunctions (e.g., *and*, *or*, *but*), articles (*a, the, an*), and short prepositions (e.g., *of, on, by, for*). The first and last words of a title must always be capitalized.

| | |
|---|---|
| *A Man for All Seasons* | *Crime and Punishment* |
| *Of Mice and Men* | *Let Me In* |
| *Rise of the West* | "What to Look For" |
| Sonata in G-Minor | "The Ever-Expanding West" |

*Strange Life of Ivan Osokin*      *Rubaiyat of Omar Khayyam*

*All in the Family*                Symphony No. 41

"Ode to Billy Joe"                Piano Concerto No. 5

## Problem Solving Example:

Proofread the following sentences for errors in capitalization. Correct any error above the line.

a. My brother said, "i'll repair the leak in the kitchen."

b. In abnormal psychology, professor Smith has all of his students check the psychology listserv on the Internet.

c. The english instructor asked his students if they had read look homeward, angel.

d. The Senator from North Carolina voted against the banking act.

e. Are you planning to join the Smith College chapter of the rotary club?

f. The President of the company spoke at my college graduation.

a. The first word in direct quotation (*I'll*) is capitalized. Also, the pronoun *I* is always capitalized.

b. *Abnormal Psychology* is capitalized because it is the name of a specific course. *Professor* is capitalized because it is a specific title that comes before a name (*Professor Smith*). *Psychology* is not capitalized because it is a general term.

c. *English* is capitalized because it is the name of a language. *Look Homeward, Angel* is capitalized because major words in the title of a work are capitalized.

d. *Senator* is not capitalized because it is a general term.

e. *Rotary Club* is capitalized because it is the name of a specific organization.

f. *President* is not capitalized because it is a general term.

## Quiz: Numbers and Capitalization

**DIRECTIONS:** Choose the correct option.

1. Mexico is the southernmost country in <u>North America</u>. It borders the United States on the north; it is bordered on the <u>south</u> by Belize and Guatemala.

   (A) north America. . .South

   (B) North America. . .South

   (C) North america. . . south

   (D) No change is necessary.

2. (A) Until 1989, Tom Landry was the only Coach the Dallas cowboys ever had.

   (B) Until 1989, Tom Landry was the only coach the Dallas Cowboys ever had.

   (C) Until 1989, Tom Landry was the only Coach the Dallas Cowboys ever had.

   (D) Until 1989, Tom Landry was the only Coach The Dallas Cowboys ever had.

3. The <u>Northern Hemisphere</u> is the half of the <u>earth</u> that lies north of the <u>Equator</u>.

   (A) Northern hemisphere. . .earth. . .equator

   (B) Northern hemisphere. . .Earth. . .Equator

   (C) Northern Hemisphere. . .earth. . .equator

   (D) No change is necessary.

4. (A) My favorite works by Ernest Hemingway are "The Snows of Kilamanjaro," *The Sun Also Rises*, and *For Whom the Bell Tolls*.

   (B) My favorite works by Ernest Hemingway are "The

Snows Of Kilamanjaro," *The Sun Also Rises*, and *For Whom The Bell Tolls.*

(C) My favorite works by Ernest Hemingway are "The Snows of Kilamanjaro," *The Sun also Rises*, and *For whom the Bell Tolls.*

(D) My favorite works by Ernest Hemingway are "The Snows of Kilamanjaro," *The Sun also Rises*, and *For Whom the Bell Tolls.*

5. Aphrodite (<u>Venus in Roman Mythology</u>) was the <u>Greek</u> goddess of love.

   (A) Venus in Roman mythology. . .greek

   (B) venus in roman mythology. . .Greek

   (C) Venus in Roman mythology. . .Greek

   (D) No change is necessary.

6. The <u>Koran</u> is considered by <u>Muslims</u> to be the holy word.

   (A) koran. . .muslims

   (B) koran. . .Muslims

   (C) Koran. . .muslims

   (D) No change is necessary.

7. (A) The freshman curriculum at the community college includes english, a foreign language, Algebra I, and history.

   (B) The freshman curriculum at the community college includes English, a foreign language, Algebra I, and history.

   (C) The Freshman curriculum at the Community College includes English, a foreign language, Algebra I, and History.

   (D) The freshman curriculum at the community college includes english, a foreign language, algebra I, and history.

8. At the <u>spring</u> graduation ceremonies, the university awarded over 2,000 <u>bachelor's</u> degrees.

   (A) Spring. . .Bachelor's

   (B) spring. . .Bachelor's

   (C) Spring. . .bachelor's

   (D) No change is necessary.

9. The fall of the <u>Berlin wall</u> was an important symbol of the collapse of <u>Communism</u>.

   (A) berlin Wall. . .communism

   (B) Berlin Wall. . .communism

   (C) berlin wall. . .communism

   (D) No change is necessary.

10. A photograph of <u>mars</u> was printed in <u>the New York Times</u>.

   (A) Mars. . .*The New York Times*

   (B) mars. . .*The New York times*

   (C) mars. . .*The New York Times*

   (D) No change is necessary.

## ANSWER KEY

| | |
|---|---|
| 1. (D) | 6. (D) |
| 2. (B) | 7. (B) |
| 3. (C) | 8. (D) |
| 4. (A) | 9. (B) |
| 5. (C) | 10. (A) |

CHAPTER **17**

## Spelling

## 17.1 Word Analysis

It is important to learn to spell properly. Poor spelling is usually a sign of haste or carelessness, and it is often taken as a sign of ignorance or illiteracy. Yet learning to spell correctly is indeed more difficult for some people than for others. In any case, it can be mastered with time and patience.

There are many helpful practices to improve spelling: using the dictionary, keeping a list of words that cause difficulty, familiarizing oneself with word origins, and studying the word list and the rules in this chapter.

A basic knowledge of the English language, especially familiarity with its numerous prefixes, can help build vocabulary and also strengthen spelling skills. For example, if one knows that *inter-* means *between* and that *intra-* means *within*, one is not likely to spell *intramural* as *intermural*. (The former means within the limits of a city, a college, etc.)

The following table lists some common Latin and Greek prefixes, which form part of the foundation of the English language.

| PREFIX | MEANING | ENGLISH EXAMPLE |
|--------|---------|-----------------|
| *ab-, a-, abs-* | away, from | abstain |

| PREFIX | MEANING | ENGLISH EXAMPLE |
|---|---|---|
| ad- | to, towards | adjacent |
| ante- | before | antecedent |
| anti- | against | antidote |
| bi- | two | bisect |
| cata-, cat-, cath- | down | cataclysm |
| circum- | round | circumlocution |
| contra- | against | contrary |
| de- | down, from | decline |
| di- | twice | diatonic |
| dis-, di- | apart, away | dissolve |
| epi-, ep-, eph- | upon, among | epidemic |
| ex-, e- | out of, from | extricate |
| hyper- | beyond, over | hyperactive |
| hypo- | under, down, less | hypodermic |
| in- | in, into | instill |
| inter- | among, between | intercede |
| intra- | within | intramural |
| meta-, met- | beyond, along with | metaphysics |
| mono- | one | monolith |
| non- | no, not | nonsense |
| ob- | against | obstruct |
| para-, par- | beside | parallel |
| per- | through | permeate |
| pre- | before | prehistoric |
| super- | above | superior |
| tele-, tel- | far | television |
| trans- | across | transpose |
| ultra- | beyond | ultraviolet |

## 17.2  Spelling List

### 100 Commonly Misspelled Words

There are some words that consistently give writers trouble. The list below contains about 100 words that are commonly misspelled. In studying this list, each person will find that certain words are more troublesome than others. These in particular should be reviewed.

| | | |
|---|---|---|
| accommodate | disastrous | occurring |
| achievement | effect | opinion |
| acquire | embarrass | opportunity |
| among | environment | parallel |
| apparent | exaggerate | particular |
| arguing | existence | performance |
| argument | existent | personal |
| athletics | experience | personnel |
| belief | explanation | possession |
| believe | fascinate | possible |
| beneficial | February | practical |
| benefited | height | precede |
| bureau | immediately | prejudice |
| business | interest | prepare |
| comparative | led | principal |
| conscious | lose | principle |
| controversial | losing | privilege |
| define | marriage | probably |
| definitely | mere | proceed |
| definition | necessary | procedure |
| describe | occasion | profession |
| description | occurred | professor |
| despair | occurrence | prominent |

| | | |
|---|---|---|
| pursue | separation | then |
| quiet | similar | thorough |
| receive | studying | to, too, two |
| receiving | succeed | tomorrow |
| recommend | succession | transferred |
| referring | surprise | unnecessary |
| remember | technique | villain |
| repetition | than | write |
| rhythm | their, they're | writing |
| sense | there | |
| separate | | |

As a handy reference, it is a good idea to set aside an area in a notebook to list problem words. Add to it any new words that are persistent spelling problems.

## 17.3 Spelling Rules

### 17.3.1 Prefixes

Prefixes (such as *dis-*, *mis-*, *in-*, *un-*, and *re-*) are added to words without doubling or dropping letters.

dis + appear = disappear
dis + agree = disagree
dis + service = disservice
dis + solved = dissolved
dis + appoint = disappoint
dis + satisfied = dissatisfied
mis + information = misinformation
mis + spelled = misspelled
mis + understand = misunderstand
mis + led = misled

in + capable = incapable
in + definite = indefinite
in + numerable = innumerable
un + usual = unusual
un + seen = unseen
un + named = unnamed
re + elect = reelect
re + search = research

## 17.3.2 Suffixes

When forming adverbs from adjectives ending in -*al*, the ending becomes -*ally*.

| normal | normally | real | really |
| occasional | occasionally | legal | legally |
| royal | royally | | |

Words ending in *n* keep the *n* when adding -*ness*.

| openness | stubbornness | suddenness | brazenness |

All words ending in -*ful* have only one *l*.

| cupful | cheerful |
| forgetful | doleful |
| mouthful | graceful |
| helpful | meaningful |
| spoonful | handful |

Add -*ment* without changing the root word's spelling.

adjust + ment = adjustment
develop + ment = development
amaze + ment = amazement

When a suffix beginning with a vowel is added, a word ending in a silent *e* generally drops the *e*.

*Example:*

admire + able = admirable
allure + ing -= alluring
believe + able = believable
come + ing = coming
dare + ing = daring
deplore + able = deplorable
desire + ous = desirous
explore + ation = exploration
fame + ous = famous
imagine + able = imaginable
move + able = movable
note + able = notable

However, the word retains the *e* when a suffix beginning with a consonant is added.

*Example:*

arrange + ment = arrangement
glee + ful = gleeful
like + ness = likeness
spite + ful = spiteful
time + less = timeless

With *judgment, acknowledgment,* and other words formed by adding *-ment* to a word with a *-dge* ending, the final *e* is usually dropped, although it is equally correct to retain it.

When adding *-ous* or *-able* to a word ending in *-ge* or *-ce*, keep the final *e* when adding the suffix. The *e* is retained to keep the soft sound of the *c* or *g*.

| | | |
|---|---|---|
| courageous | manageable | outrageous |
| changeable | advantageous | traceable |

### 17.3.3 IE + EI

In words with *ie* or *ei* in which the sound is ē, (long *ee*), use *i* before *e* except after *c*.

*Examples: i* before *e:*

| | | | |
|---|---|---|---|
| believe | pier | shield | wield |
| chief | priest | siege | yield |
| niece | reprieve | | |

*Examples:* Except after *c:*

| | | |
|---|---|---|
| ceiling | conceit | conceive |
| deceive | perceive | receive |

The following words are some exceptions to the rule and must be committed to memory.

| | | | |
|---|---|---|---|
| either | conscience | weird | reign |
| leisure | height | freight | weigh |
| neither | forfeit | seize | neighbor |

Except before *-ing*, the final *y* usually changes to *i*.

rely + ance = reliance

study + ing =-studying

modify + er = modifier

modify + ing = modifying

amplify + ed = amplified

amplify + er = amplifier

amplify + ing = amplifying

When preceded by a vowel, the final *y* does not change to *i*.

annoying, annoyed

destroying, destroyed, destroyer

journeyman, journeyed, journeyer

### 17.3.4 Doubling the Final Consonant

In one-syllable words that end in a single consonant preceded by a single vowel, double the final consonant before adding a suffix that begins with a vowel.

drop + ing = drop(p)ing

clap + ed -= clap(p)ed

man + ish = man(n)ish

snap + ed = snap(p)ed

quit + ing = quit(t)ing

However, when a suffix begins with a consonant, do not double the final consonant before adding the suffix.

man + hood = manhood

glad + ly = gladly

fat + ness = fatness

sin + ful = sinful

This is also the case in multisyllabic words that are accented on the final syllable and have endings as described above.

admit + ed = admit(t)ed

begin + ing = begin(n)ing

commit + ed = commit(t)ed

       BUT

commit + ment = commitment

However, in words with this type of ending, in which the final syllable is not accented, the final consonant is not doubled.

happen + ing = happening

profit + able = profitable

comfort + ed = comforted

refer + ence = reference

confer + ence = conference

Only three words end in *ceed* in English. They are *exceed, proceed,* and *succeed.* All other "seed-sounding" words (except *supersede*) end in *cede.*

| | |
|---|---|
| intercede | recede |
| concede | accede |
| secede | precede |

## 17.4 Proofreading

The best way to improve spelling is to reread what has been written. In fact, many other writing problems can be avoided as well if the writer carefully rereads and revises. Remember, poor spelling is not something that must be lived with. With a little work, it can be greatly improved.

## Problem Solving Example:

 Proofread the following sentences for spelling and word usage errors. Correct any errors above the line. If the sentence is correct, write correct in the blank provided.

    a. _____ Paula exaggerates there arguements all the time.

    b. _____ She could not except the gift becuase it was to expenssive.

    c. _____ If you want a job, you must aply in the personal department.

    d. _____ You must arrive promptly at 10:00 a.m. for your philosophy class.

    e. _____ All of Ralph's litter sisters plan to attend the Univrsity of Michigan.

    f. _____ I beleive your going to get the accounting position at Northern Telecom.

     a. *There* should be *their. Arguements* should be *arguments.*

    b. *Except* should be *accept. Becuase* should be *because. To* should be *too. Expenssive* should be *expensive.*

c. *Aply* should be *apply. Personal* should be *personnel.*

d. All words in this sentence are spelled correctly.

e. *Litter* should be *little. Univrsity* should be *University.*

f. *Beleive* should be *believe. Your* should be *you are* or *you're.*

## Quiz: Spelling

**DIRECTIONS:** Identify the misspelled word in each set.

1. (A) probly
   (B) accommodate
   (C) acquaintance
   (D) among

2. (A) auxiliary
   (B) atheletic
   (C) beginning
   (D) awkward

3. (A) environment
   (B) existence
   (C) Febuary
   (D) daybreak

4. (A) ocassion
   (B) occurrence
   (C) omitted
   (D) fundamental

5. (A) perspiration
   (B) referring

(C) priviledge

(D) kindergarten

**DIRECTIONS:** Choose the correct option.

6. <u>Preceding</u> the <u>business</u> session, lunch will be served in a <u>separate</u> room.

(A) preceeding. . .business. . .seperate

(B) proceeding. . .bussiness. . .seperate

(C) proceeding. . .business. . .seperite

(D) No change is necessary.

7. Monte <u>inadvertently</u> left <u>several</u> of his <u>libary</u> books in the cafeteria.

(A) inadverdently. . .serveral. . .libery

(B) inadvertently. . .several. . .library

(C) inadvertentely. . .several. . .librery

(D) No change is necessary.

8. Sam wished he had more <u>liesure</u> time so he could <u>persue</u> his favorite hobbies.

(A) leisure. . .pursue

(B) liesure. . .pursue

(C) leisure. . .persue

(D) No change is necessary.

9. One of my <u>favrite</u> <u>charecters</u> in <u>litrature</u> is Bilbo from *The Hobbit*.

(A) favrite. . .characters. . .literature

(B) favorite. . .characters. . .literature

(C) favourite. . .characters. . .literature

(D) No change is necessary.

10. Even <u>tho</u> Joe was badly hurt in the <u>accidant</u>, the company said they were not <u>lible</u> for damages.

   (A)  though. . .accidant. . .libel

   (B)  though. . .accident. . .liable

   (C)  though. . .acident. . .liable

   (D)  No change is necessary.

## ANSWER KEY

| | |
|---|---|
| 1. (A) | 6. (D) |
| 2. (B) | 7. (B) |
| 3. (C) | 8. (A) |
| 4. (A) | 9. (B) |
| 5. (C) | 10. (B) |

# NOTES

# NOTES

# NOTES

# NOTES

# NOTES

# NOTES

# NOTES

# NOTES

# NOTES

# REA's Test Preps

## The Best in Test Preparation

- REA "Test Preps" are **far more** comprehensive than any other test preparation series
- Each book contains full-length practice tests based on the most recent exams
- **Every** type of question likely to be given on the exams is included
- Answers are accompanied by **full** and **detailed** explanations

## Some of our titles include:

**Advanced Placement Exams (APs)**
Art History
Biology
Calculus AB & BC
Chemistry
Economics
English Language & Composition
English Literature & Composition
Environmental Science
European History
French Language
Government & Politics
Human Geography
Physics
Psychology
Spanish Language
Statistics
United States History
World History

**SAT Subject Tests**
Biology E/M
Chemistry
Latin
Literature
Mathematics Level 2
Spanish
United States History
World History

**College-Level Examination Program (CLEP)**
American Government
American Literature
Biology
Calculus
Chemistry
College Algebra
College Composition
History of the United States I + II
Human Growth and Development
Introduction to Educational Psychology
Introductory Psychology
Introductory Sociology
Natural Sciences
Principles of Management
Principles of Marketing
Principles of Microeconomics
Spanish
Western Civilization I + II

**ACCUPLACER**
**ACT** - ACT Assessment
**ASVAB** - Armed Services Vocational Aptitude Battery
**CBEST** - California Basic Educational Skills Test
**CDL** - Commercial Driver License Exam
**COOP, HSPT & TACHS** - Catholic High School Admission Tests

**EMT**
**ESL**
**FTCE** - Florida Teacher Certification Examinations
**GED® Test**
**GMAT** - Graduate Management Admission Test
**GRE** - Graduate Record Exams
**LSAT** - Law School Admission Test
**MAT** - Miller Analogies Test
**MTEL** - Massachusetts Tests for Educator Licensure
**NCLEX**
**NYSTCE** - New York State Teacher Certification Examinations
**PRAXIS**
**SAT**
**TEAS**
**TExES** - Texas Examinations of Educator Standards
**TOEFL** - Test of English as a Foreign Language

*For our complete title list,*
*visit www.rea.com*

**Research & Education Association**